THE
NEW
DAD
DICTIONARY

THE
NEW
DAD
DICTIONARY

EVERYTHING HE REALLY NEEDS TO KNOW—FROM A TO Z

CHRIS ILLUMINATI

AVON, MASSACHUSETTS

Published by
Adams Media, a division of F+W Media, Inc.
57 Littlefield Street, Avon, MA 02322. U.S.A.
www.adamsmedia.com

ISBN 10: 1-4405-8523-7
ISBN 13: 978-1-4405-8523-4
eISBN 10: 1-4405-8524-5
eISBN 13: 978-1-4405-8524-1

Printed in the United States of America.

10 9 8 7 6 5 4 3 2 1

Library of Congress Cataloging-in-Publication Data

Illuminati, Chris.
The new dad dictionary / Chris Illuminati.
    pages cm
Includes index.
ISBN 978-1-4405-8523-4 (pob) -- ISBN 1-4405-8523-7 (pob) -- ISBN 978-1-4405-
8524-1 (ebook) -- ISBN 1-4405-8524-5 (ebook)
1. Fatherhood. 2. Parenthood. 3. Pregnancy. 4. Child rearing. I. Title.
HQ756.I43 2015
306.874'2--dc23
                                      2014045314

Cover design by Sylvia McArdle.
Cover images © Clipart.com.

This book is available at quantity discounts for bulk purchases.
For information, please call 1-800-289-0963.

To my "bud" Evan and my "bean" Lyla—
I love you both more than I can explain.

To my Permanent Roommate—without you, I'm lost.
Literally, lost. Is this the kitchen? I love you very much.

ACKNOWLEDGMENTS

This is my third book. It's time to start acknowledging specific people instead of lumping everyone together as family, friends, and people to whom I owe money.

A huge thank you to Brendan O'Neill at Adams for once again believing that people would want to read my work, and to my agent, Andrea Barzvi for believing that people will want to read my work for a very long time.

A humble thank you to friends new and old who've stuck with and by me through it all, especially Don Povia and Frank Martini.

A heartfelt thank you to my family, both blood and by marriage, who shaped me into the man I am today: Aunt Ro, Tommy, Brenda, Matt, Erin, Mary, Tom, Susan, Big Susan, and especially Uncle Frank, Uncle Larry, Nanny, and Grandpa watching from somewhere above.

And last but never least, the biggest gratitude to all of my parents—Fran and Tony Illuminati. Thank you. I love you both.

CONTENTS

PART 3: THE REST OF YOUR LIFE • 137

INTRODUCTION

So you're a new dad or are about to become a new dad. Congratulations! But before you pat yourself on the back too wholeheartedly, you probably want to answer some questions:

- When your partner says she doesn't want an episiotomy, do you know what that means?
- Do you know how to handle meconium or jaundice?
- Are you going to be an authoritarian parent or an authoritative parent? A snowplow parent or a helicopter parent?

If you're not sure how to answer these questions or don't even know what meconium is, don't worry. *The New Dad Dictionary* gives you everything you need to know to talk the talk of new parenthood. You see, I've been there and know how hard it is to raise a child or sit through your partner's appointment with her obstetrician when you don't even know the words that are coming out of the doctor's mouth.

In April 2010, I quit my job to raise my one-month-old son. I'm a writer, so after suffering sticker shock at the amount of money someone else wanted to watch my kid, I figured I'd watch my own kid—thank you very much—lined up some freelance writing work to bring in some income, and became a stay-at-home dad. On trips to the doctor, days at the public playground, and just hanging out bullshitting with other parents, I've heard all the words you need to know—and I learned the hard way. I'd do the same thing every time the pediatrician mentioned croup or another parent said he was redshirting his child this year. I'd nod my head and say, "Totally, totally," then either ask my wife what the hell it meant (she always knew the answer so I felt better that at least one of us took this parenting gig seriously) or I'd look the term up online or in one of the countless child-rearing books gifted to us that I never took the time to read. The problem was that the answers, all the common terms and definitions, were scattered across numerous texts, the Internet, and various message boards. There wasn't a single, handy resource to pick up and leaf through for my queries about the Ferber method, au pairs, and separation anxiety. Those minutes, hours, and days of research inspired *The New Dad Dictionary*.

Throughout the book, you'll find 150 quick definitions for the most popular and prevalent parenting terms. Each term is broken down into a Definition, a textbook explanation of the term, and a Dadfinition, an interpretation of the definition that's based on my personal experience and research and put into straightforward language for other dads (or dudes) to understand.

And no matter where you are in parenthood, you'll find what you need to know within these pages. The book is broken down into three sections that cover everything from the pregnancy terms that will pop up in every conversation with your spouse to toddler terms to buzzwords and phrases that will bombard you as the parent of a young child. You'll also find info on various types of parenting styles, toys, and role-playing, as well as all the little tricks to keep your kid safe and you sane. As sane as possible, anyway.

So as you move forward in parenthood, keep in mind that caring for the actual tiny human being is simple. Being prepared, and educated, about all the other stuff is the challenge. Good luck!

PART 1

PREGNANCY

Pregnancy is an amazing, exciting, and joyous event in a woman's life. Being with child for nine months is by no means easy, but a woman will learn a tremendous amount about herself. Pregnancy will be all those things for you, too, except you'll spend the whole time secretly freaking the hell out.

You're going to be a dad. It's going to change your life in a thousand ways. It's going to alter your emotions, change your opinions, and reshape how you see the world. You're also going to come across a slew of new terms, like *hospital tour* and *trimesters*, that will make your head spin like the mobile hanging above your soon-to-be-born child's crib.

In this section of the book, you'll learn the most common pregnancy terms. Memorize the definitions so you can have a conversation with your pregnant partner . . . because you're not going to be talking about anything else for the next nine months.

AMNIOCENTESIS

DEFINITION

Amniocentesis is a prenatal test where doctors use a fine needle to remove a small amount of the amniotic fluid that surrounds the fetus. The needle is inserted into the uterus, through the abdomen, with help from an ultrasound as guidance. Amniotic fluid contains live fetal skin cells and other substances that hold valuable information about the baby's health prior to birth.

Amniocentesis is often performed on mothers between 15–20 weeks pregnant who will be thirty-five and older at the time of delivery. Amniocentesis is also often performed on pregnant women with a family history of children born with birth defects, as well as on women who received abnormal results in other prenatal tests to detect certain types of birth defects.

DADFINITION

Amniocentesis—"amnio" for short, because the last thing new parents have time for is to say long words—is just one of the never-ending prenatal tests your partner may have to endure during pregnancy.

If amniocentesis is necessary, you may want to accompany your partner to the appointment. This particular procedure is uncomfortable and comes with a few after effects such as minor cramps and soreness. That said, you really should be going to all of her prenatal appointments. The poor woman is going to get poked, prodded, and put into myriad odd situations at the doctor's office. She'll want you there for support or just to punch for putting her through all this crap. Wear thick clothing; the punches sting less.

ASSISTED BIRTH

DEFINITION

Assisted birth refers to a variety of procedures that help the child come out of the vagina. The procedures utilize instruments—either forceps or ventouse suction cup—that attach to the child's head.

Forceps, which look like tongs, can be used to grab, maneuver, or remove the baby either within or from the body. A ventouse delivery involves the use of a vacuum-like device to remove the baby from the uterus when the second stage of labor has not adequately progressed.

During delivery, the attending physician will recommend an assisted birth if the woman has been pushing for an extended period of time, to the point of exhaustion, or if the baby is nearly out but his heart rate is low.

DADFINITION

Assisted birth is just proof that even the most brilliant doctors, at one point or another, fell back on manly instincts to get the job done.

Oh sure, when you offered to get the kid out using a pair of salad tongs or a vacuum cleaner, you were being "insensitive" or making light of a serious situation. As soon as the guy with the medical degree offers these options, your partner jumps all over the idea. Apparently saying, "This kid is being rather uncooperative in this whole experience. We'll need to remove him. Do we have any pliers or a vacuum cleaner handy?" is only appreciated when uttered by a medical professional. Who knew?

BABY CONCIERGE

DEFINITION

A baby concierge is a service for expecting parents that handles all of the things that a pregnant woman needs to do to prepare for her baby's arrival.

Expectant mothers often feel unprepared and overwhelmed with all of the loose ends that must be tied up before the baby arrives. Adding to the pressure is the feeling that once the child is born, there will be little free time to get anything done. A baby concierge plans, prepares, gives advice, and supports a family to alleviate unnecessary stresses on the expectant mom.

Baby concierges can also help parents register for baby items; design, organize, and set up a nursery; find a pediatrician; name a baby; plan a baby shower; and organize any other activity.

DADFINITION

A baby concierge is a service for expecting moms who don't have any other women in their lives, don't have access to the Internet or a telephone, or watch too much Bravo and think it's real life.

There is nothing experienced moms love more than helping expectant moms to avoid all the mistakes they made before their babies were born. Moms live to give advice to other moms. Dads get a kick out of it, too. If a pregnant woman needs help, all she has to do is ask another woman, not a service charging anywhere from $100–$300 dollars or more *per hour*.

Don't get me wrong, a baby concierge is a sweet gig, preying on the insecurities of expectant and hormonal mothers with a "sky is falling" approach, fearful that their baby's future bedroom might be saddled with bad feng shui.

Or maybe I'm just bitter because I didn't think of the idea first.

BIRTHING BALL

DEFINITION

A birthing ball is a large air-filled rubber ball that a pregnant woman can sit on during labor. Using a birthing ball can help a pregnant woman move into different upright positions while remaining supported, which can make labor easier and may even shorten labor by an hour or more.

Birthing balls also come in handy during the later stages of pregnancy. Women typically use them to sit comfortably while working or relaxing because they're easier to get on and off of than a stationary chair. A birthing ball is also perfect for gentle exercises and improving posture and balance. It can even help change the position of a baby in a breech presentation later in the pregnancy.

DADFINITION

A birthing ball is a ball that used to live in your home gym but now takes up space in the living room. It was once vital in giving you six-pack abs, but now your pregnant partner rolls around on it like she's drunk on a six-pack of beer.

After birth, the ball is perfect for staring at while both you and your partner promise you'll start working out. Eventually, the ball goes back to live in the basement among the dusty barbells and hundreds of rolls of wrapping paper that will never get used. The birthing ball may be passed down to your child to be used as exercise equipment or can also be thrown in the backyard to keep the dog—or the baby—occupied for hours on end.

BIRTH PLAN

DEFINITION

A birth plan is a document that tells a pregnant woman's medical team her preferences during labor and delivery and postpartum. It may contain her wishes for things such as how to manage labor pain or whether she'd like to have skin-to-skin contact with the baby right after delivery.

The mother-to-be should give a copy of her birth plan to everyone involved in the birth, ranging from the doctor to the doula to the nurses. However, since unexpected situations commonly come up during labor, she should tell the doctors what she wants but remain flexible.

You and your partner shouldn't wait until the last minute to put together a birth plan and should share the plan with her doctor a few weeks before delivery. Discussing her wishes ahead of time will help your partner open a line of communication with her ob-gyn.

DADFINITION

Birth plans are a road map for an agreeable pregnancy for a mom. Dads don't have a birth plan, but if they did, it would look like this:

Plan on standing for a very long period of time. Plan on wearing scrubs that make you look like a walking piece of construction paper. Plan on a very agitated woman in immense pain yelling at you. Plan on being in a room and seeing things that can't be unseen. Plan on falling in love with another human in her first few seconds on Earth. Plan on crying. Plan on kissing the woman who was yelling at you for the past half-hour. No, that's the nurse. Kiss the other woman. The one who just gave birth to your child. Plan on being insanely happy.

That's every dad's birth plan.

Oh, forgot one. Plan on never sleeping again! (Insert devilish laughs and twist of a nonexistent handlebar mustache.)

BRAXTON HICKS CONTRACTIONS

DEFINITION

Braxton Hicks contractions are also called "practice contractions" because they prepare the woman, both physically and mentally, for the real event of childbirth and allow her to practice her breathing exercises and the coming sensations of labor.

Named after a prominent English physician who practiced in the late 1800s, Braxton Hicks contractions occur when the muscles of the uterus tighten for anywhere from 30 seconds to around 1–2 minutes.

Braxton Hicks contractions can begin as early as the second trimester but are most commonly experienced in the third trimester.

DADFINITION

Braxton Hicks contractions are the lame duck wide receivers of the pregnancy world.

Imagine Braxton Hicks as a blue-chip wide receiver from an SEC school—the kid with the sure hands who goes top five in the NFL draft. You pick him in the late rounds of your fantasy draft because he's already been named a starter. Week one of the season Hicks puts up gaudy numbers for a rookie so you insert him in your lineup week two where he does absolutely nothing. You rotate him in and out of your lineup for weeks, but he always scores a ton of points on your bench but nets a big fat zero in your starting lineup.

Braxton Hicks the imaginary football player is a damn tease. Braxton Hicks the contractions aren't much different. Every day closer to labor your partner is going to tell you, *"This is the day!"* because her body is tricking her into thinking the child is on his way out. When this happens, tell her the story of the fictional Braxton Hicks. She could probably use the nap.

BREECH PRESENTATION

DEFINITION

When babies are aligned in the uterus to come out butt first as opposed to head first—which is the safest way for babies to be born—it is called a breech presentation.

During a typical delivery, the head, which is the largest part of a baby, passes out of the birth canal first. In a breech presentation, the baby's hips come out first and may not adequately open up the birth canal enough to allow the head to pass through, which can cause the head to become stuck in the birth canal. Because of the dangers associated with a breech birth, most breech babies are delivered by cesarean section.

DADFINITION

A breech presentation won't be the first time in your baby's life that he leads with his ass. He'll spend most of his teens doing the exact same thing. Unlike the delivery room doctor, who might make an attempt to turn the baby's head down by pushing down strategically on your partner's abdomen, you'll need to push him in different ways.

Breech presentation is a common occurrence, and a cesarean section, though still considered a major surgery, is a normal procedure in delivery rooms around the country. There is no reason to worry unless the doctor tells you there is reason to worry.

CERVIX DILATION AND EFFACEMENT

DEFINITION

Dilation is the opening of the cervix, and effacement is the thinning of the cervix. The dilation is measured in centimeters, while effacement is measured in percentage.

The two processes mean a pregnant woman is getting closer to giving birth as they work together to create a pathway from the uterus to the birth canal that the child will travel during labor.

The timing of these processes is different for every woman. For some, dilation and effacement happens gradually and can take weeks, while some pregnant women will dilate and efface overnight.

DADFINITION

Dilation and effacement are the body's way of announcing, "Get ready, lady. Labor is right around the corner."

Cervix dilation and effacement is the two-minute warning of pregnancy. The game is almost over. Either you're on defense—ready at any moment with packed bags and painted nurseries—or on offense and preparing for the birth of a child in what feels like 120 seconds.

The dilation does take some time—unless the kid is in a hurry to see her unpainted room—so even if your partner feels like she's ready, it might be a couple of weeks until the big moment. It's probably the only time in your life that you'll be incredibly consumed with measuring using the metric system.

CESAREAN SECTION, C-SECTION

DEFINITION

A cesarean section, or C-section, is the procedure done to surgically deliver a baby through the abdomen of the mother.

In the United States, about one in four women deliver their babies via C-section. The majority of C-sections are performed unexpectedly when labor and delivery don't go according to plan, but some are scheduled when issues with delivery are known ahead of time. Potential problems that may cause a C-section to be performed include various health problems of the mother, the positioning of the baby inside the womb, insufficient room for the baby to pass through the vagina, or signs of fetal distress. Mothers who have had previous C-sections are also candidates. This procedure is also common among women who are carrying multiple babies.

DADFINITION

A cesarean section is probably the only time you'll ever be in an operating room without being the one sliced open. This makes for a pretty surreal situation. Yes, you're excited about the pending birth of your child, but, oh yeah, your partner is laid out on a table and opened wider than a Florida sinkhole.

Just keep your eyes focused on your partner, your kid, or at the tops of your shoes, and you won't see anything you probably don't want to see.

Both of my kids were delivered via cesarean section. The first was unexpected due to a variety of complications and the second was planned, much like a nail appointment: "What are you doing on the twentieth, doc? Nothing? Want to take the kid out of my stomach? Great, see ya then. Dress accordingly."

DOULA

DEFINITION

A doula is any nonmedical person who assists a woman before, during, and after childbirth. He or she also helps the husband and family by providing physical and emotional support during pregnancy and in the first few weeks of childbirth, or longer as the family desires.

Some of the responsibilities of a doula during childbirth include understanding the physiology of birth and the emotional needs of a woman in labor, assisting the woman in carrying out her birth plan, staying with the woman throughout labor, providing emotional support and physical comfort, and assisting mom with getting all the information she needs to make informed decisions.

DADFINITION

A doula is another helping hand in the chaotic time known as pregnancy and childbirth.

Pregnancy, labor, and parenthood are amazing and scary endeavors. It doesn't hurt to have a person, like a doula, who's seen it all a hundred times and can help out with not only supporting a woman through labor but in the days after the big game.

The role of the doula isn't to take your place in this big birthing plan. Think of labor as the Super Bowl, your pregnant partner is the head coach, the doula is the assistant coach, and you're one of the coordinators. Let the coach and the head coach draw up the game plan and run it on Super Bowl Sunday. You still get all of the benefits of being on the winning team.

Another way to think of it is to imagine you're the right hand and the doula is the left hand, and both hands are needed during pregnancy. Just try not to high-five too much; those hands need to be free to do a hundred other things.

DROPPING

DEFINITION

"Dropping" is the term for the moving of the fetus to the lower part of the abdomen when he settles his head into the pelvis as preparation for birth.

Expectant moms who have "dropped" will notice that their abdomen hangs lower than it did in the previous weeks. Some moms are even able to feel or sense the baby's head resting just under the middle of the pelvic bone. When seated, it will feel to the pregnant woman as though the baby is on her lap. Even if mom doesn't notice the change, other people will usually notice the difference and make comments about the baby dropping into place and being ready for the pending birth.

DADFINITION

Dropping is when your partner's pregnant belly sags lower and you pretend to notice.

While everyone else takes notice of your pregnant partner's suddenly lower hanging belly, you'll probably be the last to notice—if you even notice at all.

If you don't notice a change in her stomach, it's fine. You're not alone. If she asks, "Haven't you noticed in a change in the way I'm carrying?" Just say, "Yes, of course," and assume she means dropping. There's an outside shot she's referring to the way she's carrying objects because her stomach has grown so massive she can't lift, bend, squat, or make any movement without waddling.

Speaking of dropping, the third trimester is around the time your own stomach will drop. You'll probably feel all those late-night feasts as those sympathy snacks—because you can't let her eat pizza alone!—drop close down to your pelvis.

EPIDURAL

DEFINITION

An epidural, medically known as epidural anesthesia, is a regional anesthetic injected into the lower back. The medicine blocks the pain signals sent from the nerves that are agitated by labor.

Epidurals, the most popular tool for pain relief during labor and delivery, provide women with localized pain relief, which allows them to still feel movement and contractions.

DADFINITION

Epidurals are the injections that many pregnant women say they don't want until they're actually in labor.

Many women chose to forgo the epidural, especially during natural childbirth. If mom's not going to use it and the needle is in close proximity, maybe they could give it to you? I'm all for anything that makes delivery easier for everyone involved. After all, you're the one who's going to be standing during delivery for hours and then spending a few nights on a hospital flip chair to help care for the newborn. You deserve a little pain relief!

EPISIOTOMY

DEFINITION

An episiotomy is the surgical process of enlarging the vaginal opening with a cut to the perineum, the area between the vagina and the anus.

Episiotomies were once routine procedures done just before delivery to help speed delivery along and prevent the vagina from tearing. The belief was that a clean incision would heal quicker than a spontaneous tear, but recent studies have shown that this is not the case. Episiotomies are still done today in certain circumstances.

DADFINITION

An episiotomy is one of the wince-inducing parts of labor that you—and your partner—would rather forget.

The procedures that accompany childbirth are ever changing. They're much different now than when you were born and will continue to change and evolve as technology changes and more research is done on the long-term effects of birthing procedures. In the not-too-distant future there will hopefully come an end to any unnecessary slicing, tearing, clipping, and stripping of the human body when delivering a kid. Eventually humans will figure out a way to just have the child delivered via UPS. Rather than listen to someone recount a horrific labor story, imagine how much nicer it would be to hear, "There's a note on the door. We must have missed a delivery. Oh, damn it, it was our new son! It says they'll try again tomorrow. I've just got to sign this slip and they'll leave him on the back porch."

FAMILY MEDICAL HISTORY

DEFINITION

A family medical history is the record of the health information of a child's relatives. Doctors typically ask for a family medical history when seeing new patients and consider a complete history to be one that includes info going back through three generations of direct relatives.

Genes are passed down through generations of family members, which means that many diseases or health issues are hereditary. A child is more likely to develop a health problem if someone else in the family has experienced that health problem as well. By referencing a family medical history, doctors are able to see if a child may have an increased risk of developing a certain medical issue and are able to treat the patient accordingly.

DADFINITION

If you ever want to worry about the genetic baggage that you've passed down to your kid, a family medical history is a good place to start looking.

A family medical history is a detailed (as much as possible) record of every medical ailment in your family dating as far back as humanely possible. If you have an open family, a medical history is easy to obtain. If you have a family that hides everything, you're going to have to do some verbal probing.

After you've uncovered every family disease and ailment dating back to the Great Depression, it's not a bad idea to sit down and take a quick inventory of your own medical issues and visits to the doctor. There's a good chance they'll have a connection to a medical issue your kid is having now or will suffer down the road.

It's impossible to remember every ailment that you've ever gone to the doctor for, so take this opportunity to get a physical exam for yourself (you have to take better care of yourself now that there are kids involved) and ask the doctor to briefly go over all the reasons for your visits in the last ten years. They're all at your doctor's fingertips in that little laptop she lugs around from room to room. Did you think your doctor was playing first-person shooter games on that thing all day?

FETUS

DEFINITION

The fetus is the unborn person or animal in the womb. The term "fetus" is used to describe a being in the later stages of development after the body structures—such as the arms, legs, fingers, toes, ears, and eyelids—are in recognizable form. Before a fetus becomes a fetus, at the end of the eighth week, it is an embryo.

Throughout the fetal period of a pregnancy, the fetus continues to grow and develop. During this time period, the lungs develop, the features of the face become fully formed (during weeks 9–12), and the fetus becomes able to make and release a fist with its hand. During this time, the fetus also closes its eyelids and keeps them closed until the pregnancy is nearly over, which allows the retina to develop correctly.

DADFINITION

The fetus is the unborn child living inside the womb without a care in the world. You and mom are doing all of the worrying.

People believe a lot of things begin during the fetal stage of pregnancy, like parenting. You're not caring for the kid yet (mom's body is doing that with little help from you), but you're preparing for the kid, worrying about the kid inside the womb and what's going to happen when he or she eventually pops out, and even staring at the sonogram photos and thinking about a hundred different moments that are yet to come.

The fetal stage of development is the only time as a parent you'll feel the kid is at least 90 percent safe, but that's not going to stop you from worrying anyway. Welcome to parenthood.

FOOD CRAVINGS

DEFINITION

Food cravings happen often in the early stages of pregnancy and usually last throughout the nine months. Food cravings are the sudden urge for a particular food, type of food, or dish. A large majority of pregnant women (and some dads-to-be) experience food cravings.

Pregnant women tend to experience food cravings during the early part of pregnancy because their bodies are attempting to adjust to the pregnancy hormones. Besides food cravings, most pregnant women find that there's at least one previously loved item of food that they can longer tolerate.

DADFINITION

Food cravings are the sudden urge for a particular edible item that isn't in the house, or likely might not exist, but you better find it fast or your partner is going to lose her mind.

One time when my wife was pregnant, she found herself craving McDonald's and wanted more than just a few items off their menu. I picked up her food, brought it home, and set it on the dining room table. After checking over the

---

FICTIONAL BUT FUNNY

PREGNANCY BRAIN

A phenomenon that overtakes pregnant women, usually in the second trimester, that causes women to become unusually disorganized and forgetful. When a woman suffers from pregnancy brain it is believed that the baby is sucking all mom's brain power. This is believed by frustrated men only.

order she looked up and asked, "Where's yours?" I replied, "I'm not really hungry." I learned that day to never let a pregnant woman eat alone. Apparently hormones affect more than just food cravings, so be prepared to partake in every meal—no matter how big or how crazy—with your pregnant partner.

FULL-TERM PREGNANCY

DEFINITION

The term "full-term pregnancy" refers to a pregnancy that ends at between 39 and 40 weeks.

In 2013, the definition of what constitutes a full-term pregnancy changed when the journal *Obstetrics & Gynecology* published new accepted guidelines for ob-gyns. Today's standards break down the terminology as follows:

- Early term: between 37 weeks and 38 weeks and 6 days
- Full term: between 39 weeks and 40 weeks and 6 days
- Late term: the 41st week
- Post term: after 42 weeks

A full-term pregnancy is ideal for the baby for a variety of health reasons, including decreased mortality rates and increased development.

DADFINITION

Full-term pregnancy is a baby getting his money's worth out of the temporary place he's calling home.

The body is a crazy thing. Add to it another human body and things get even nuttier. A body not ready to make its exit into the world collides with a body ready to push it out as soon as possible. The irresistible force meets the doesn't-want-to-be-movable object. Don't worry, this isn't the last time that mom and baby are going to butt heads on a topic.

The baby will come out when he's good and ready or when mom's body decides "All right, that's about enough!" and starts moving things along. All you can really do is wait.

HOSPITAL BAG

DEFINITION

A hospital bag is a travel bag packed in preparation of the pending birth of a baby.

Experts recommend packing two small bags for the hospital. The first bag should contain items a woman will need before or during labor, and the second bag should contain items a woman will need after the birth. Some of the most important items to pack include:

- Picture ID (for hospital admission purposes)
- Insurance card
- Hospital paperwork
- Birth plan
- Bathrobe
- Sleepwear
- Slippers
- Toiletries
- Clothes for mom to go home in
- An outfit for the baby to go home in

Mom should also pack any necessities that will make her comfortable and whatever she uses at home to relax.

The hospital bag should be packed around the eighth month of pregnancy since a woman go can go into labor at any time and there may not be time to pack a bag.

DADFINITION

A hospital bag is a travel bag packed in preparation for birth, but it will never have everything a woman needs, so you should prepare to run to the store or to the house a hundred times.

Unless a woman has had a recent hospital visit—and hopefully she hasn't—there's no perfect way to prepare. It's almost like taking a vacation. There are so many incidentals that it's almost impossible to pack everything you're going to need. Get ready to bring a third bag from home with all of the stuff she forgot or didn't know she should pack.

Be sure to pack a bag for yourself as well. Remember to bring clothes to sleep and lounge around in, toiletries, electronics to record the birth or the first days with the baby, and the most important item of all—a pair of comfortable shoes.

HOSPITAL TOUR

DEFINITION

A hospital tour is a guided tour around the facility in which a pregnancy woman will be giving birth.

During the hospital tour, a delivery nurse or hospital educator will walk expecting parents through the whole delivery process—from admission to discharge—and will explain the options available to the family. Stops on the tour should include the triage area, the family waiting rooms, a labor and delivery room, the postpartum room, and the floor where the mother and child will stay until their release.

A good time to tour the hospital is between week 30 and week 34 of pregnancy. If considering several options or hospitals, it's best to schedule the first tour a few weeks earlier.

DADFINITION

A hospital tour is a half-hour journey through the facility that will deliver your child, during which a plethora of information will be thrown your way, of which you'll remember little a month later when checking in to give birth.

There are a few questions you should ask while on hospital tours, including where dads sleep at night and on what, how late the cafeteria is open, what the policy is on bringing in outside food, visiting hours for family, and how good the cable is in the rooms.

You should also introduce yourself to all the nurses on the floor as "the guy who'll be wandering the halls at night either looking for something to do or something to eat." Instruct the nurse that if she should find you babbling incoherently and walking in circles late at night to just hand you a Snickers bar and point you back toward your family.

INCUBATOR

DEFINITION

Incubators, sometimes called isolettes, are enclosed, heated, plastic bassinets used to give sufficient warmth to babies born prematurely. Incubators are primarily used in neonatal intensive care units (NICU). Infants cared for in incubators are also given needed respiratory support ranging from extra oxygen to mechanical ventilation as needed.

A transport incubator is a movable unit used when a sick or premature baby is being transported from one hospital to another. Transport incubators usually have a cardiorespiratory monitor, miniature ventilator, pulse oximeter, oxygen supply, and IV pump built into its frame.

DADFINITION

Incubators are pieces of medical equipment that you're thankful exist but you hope you never need to see one up close.

If your baby is in an incubator, chances are you'll be spending a lot of time in the neonatal intensive care unit, which can be a scary place. Thankfully, advances in technology and modern medicine mean the child will get the best care and attention at this crucial time.

INDUCED LABOR

DEFINITION

Induced labor is the act of bringing on labor even if a woman's body isn't necessarily ready.

If labor doesn't begin on its own and the ob-gyn feels that it's medically necessary to induce, the doctor will likely use a combination of medications and other techniques to kick-start labor. The practitioner can also use some of these same methods to restart stalled labor as needed. Induction is typically recommended when a pregnant woman goes one or two weeks past her due date.

DADFINITION

"Induced labor" is the medical term for "getting the birth show on the road."

A kid wants to make her grand entrance into the world on her timetable. It's only natural after a nine-month buildup. But there are times when, for the health and safety of everyone involved, the wheels need to get moving on the entire labor.

The kid can still make a big entrance during an induced labor—maybe a laser show in the delivery room or backflip out of the mom's stomach—but if mom has to wait any longer, she might be the one doing backflips in the delivery room.

There are "home techniques" that may be used to get the labor process moving, such as sexual intercourse or nipple stimulation, but neither have been proven effective. They've been proven awesome, but not effective. So if your partner's doctor recommends induction, give these methods a try, but then let the professionals take it from there.

LABOR

DEFINITION

Labor is the process through which the baby and the placenta are removed from the uterus.

Labor occurs in three stages that begin weeks before a woman gives birth:

- The first stage begins with the woman's first mild contractions, which can begin weeks before she actually gives birth. This first stage continues until her cervix dilates or stretches to a full 10 centimeters (about 4 inches).
- The second stage is called the active stage. As its name suggests, during this stage the woman begins to push. This stage ends with the birth of the baby.
- The third stage starts when the baby has been delivered and ends with the delivery of the placenta and afterbirth.

DADFINITION

Labor is a pretty scary thing. The good thing is that the first and the third stages of labor really have nothing to do with you. The second stage is where you really get involved in the delivery of the child.

Don't worry, the doctor isn't going to ask you to lend a hand, but you'll hopefully be in the delivery room as an active participant. Even if you don't remember how to coach your partner on how to breathe, or when to push, she'll still appreciate you holding her hand and being nice when she yells at you.

One word about labor though: Be careful where your eyes roam. Some things just can't be unseen.

LAMAZE

DEFINITION

Lamaze is a childbirth technique that uses both physical and breathing exercises to provide relief to a woman during labor instead of administering drugs. In Lamaze, women are taught a variety of simple coping strategies including breathing, massage, walking, and position changes.

The Lamaze method of childbirth, developed by the French obstetrician Fernand Lamaze, is one of the most commonly taught childbirth classes. In the early days of Lamaze coaching, the focus was on using controlled breathing techniques to cope with labor, but the vision has since expanded in an effort to increase a woman's confidence in her ability to give birth.

DADFINITION

Lamaze teaches you and your partner a variety of birthing techniques that you may forget as soon as you get to the hospital. That's not to say that Lamaze, or birthing, classes aren't helpful. They generally devote one full session to just the fathers as a way to not only prepare them for the birth but to explain how they can be helpful during the most painful experience in their partner's life. It's also a good spot for fathers to ask questions about the process of labor and what to expect when the doctor calls you into the delivery room.

A key component to the Lamaze technique involves an increased role of the male during labor, because why should she have all the fun? Kidding. It's because for a long time men just stood there and did nothing while the woman did all the heavy lifting. After all, you're part of the reason she's in this mess, so you better be there to bail her out.

MIDWIFE

DEFINITION

A midwife is a medical professional who assists the mother during labor and delivery either in the hospital or birthing center or for a home birth.

Many of today's midwives have had formal training as nurses and then had specialized training in midwifery. Midwives also have a relationship with obstetricians who provide consultation during labor if needed. The midwife may refer a woman to an obstetrician for care if a problem develops during the pregnancy and can also team up with another midwife or doula (an assistant who provides nonmedical care) to help with your partner's labor and delivery.

DADFINITION

A midwife is one more person in the world qualified to deliver your baby. It will start to feel like everyone on Earth is specialized in delivering babies. It's almost like the trend where everyone is an ordained minister and can perform a wedding ceremony.

If you choose to use a midwife, make sure he or she is certified and that you have a plan in place in case your partner or your baby need emergency medical care. Be sure to double-check the double checks.

I once made a joke during a birthing class that a midwife sounded like the wife between the first wife and the last wife. Never make this joke in a room full of temperamental pregnant women. You're welcome.

MORNING SICKNESS

DEFINITION

Nausea gravidarum, better known as morning sickness, refers to the nausea and vomiting that typically occurs in the first trimester of pregnancy. Morning sickness usually affects half of all pregnant women.

Medical experts consider the term "morning sickness" a misnomer since many pregnant women experience morning sickness most of the day and sometimes into the evening.

The symptoms of morning sickness include a constant feeling of nausea, vomiting, and sluggishness. Symptoms may get severe to the point of dehydration, hypokalemia (low blood potassium), alkalosis (a dangerous drop in the normal acidity of the blood), and weight loss.

DADFINITION

Morning sickness is a fantastic side effect of pregnancy that will make both you and your partner miserable for at least a few months. She'll be sick of being sick and tired, and you'll be sick and tired of her being sick. No matter how bad it gets, be nice, because there's no reason to agitate a vomiting woman.

There are simple remedies to help ease the nausea and vomiting—pressure bands for the wrists and ginger candies seem to work well for some—but the best remedy is just to weather the storm. As with everything in pregnancy, this too shall pass (for most women), and the ailments will subside as fast as they developed.

Ironically, there will come a point in your life where you'd gladly trade the early morning cries of a newborn for the sounds of a pregnant woman tossing cookies in the bathroom. Truth.

NATURAL CHILDBIRTH

DEFINITION

Natural childbirth is the act of giving birth without the use of an epidural or other medication for pain relief and without any invasive, surgical procedures like an episiotomy. Natural childbirth allows the laboring woman (and her partner) to remain in control and lead the labor and delivery process, dealing with it any way in which she is comfortable.

Women who choose natural childbirth often want to connect to the experience of labor and delivery and may believe that the female body is already equipped to handle this experience without intervention. In addition, some women choose natural childbirth as a way to avoid the risks that pain medication may cause the baby or themselves. Pain medications can affect labor by altering a woman's blood pressure and making her feel nauseous and out of control in the situation.

DADFINITION

Natural childbirth is pretty much one of the most insane things your partner will ever do.

Think about it. She has the benefits of modern medicine at her fingertips (or the fingertips of her doctor and anesthesiologist), but she's kicking modern science to the curb and making labor and delivery her bitch. Unreal.

Abstaining from drugs during childbirth isn't a new concept, and I applaud women for it. If your partner decides to go this route, get ready to be pretty overwhelmed—and really freakin' impressed.

NESTING

DEFINITION

Nesting during pregnancy describes the overwhelming urge of the mother-to-be to get the house ready for the pending arrival of a newborn.

The nesting urge can be brought on by several different factors including the boredom and frustration of still being pregnant, the recognition that the baby will take up a majority of a woman's time and energy, or just the nervous energy and excitement that comes with such a life change.

The nesting instinct is strongest in women in the latter weeks of pregnancy, usually during the third trimester. It is an old wives' tale that once a pregnant woman begins to feel the urge to nest that labor is just around the corner.

DADFINITION

Nesting is the urge of the pregnant woman to thoroughly clean and declutter your entire house at a point in her pregnancy when she can no longer lift any heavy objects or use any potentially harmful cleaners. This means that her urge to nest equates to more work around the house for you. If you're lucky, she'll do most of the cleaning, arranging, and room swapping with her mother or sister while you play with the furniture layout to give the room feng shui.

While you may have been an unwilling participant in the past, it is now in your best interest to agree that every room needs to be painted, every closet cleaned, and every nook and cranny of the house look picture-perfect. When she finally falls asleep at night, hide all your precious belongings in the garage and don't bring them back in the house until the child is born. In her tired and delusional days caring for a newborn baby she won't have the energy to argue that Stormtrooper helmets don't belong in a guest bathroom.

OBSTETRICIAN

DEFINITION

An obstetrician is a physician who specializes in pregnancy, labor, and the postpartum time period following childbirth. Most obstetricians are also trained gynecologists, physicians who specialize in the female reproductive system. Typically, the education and training for both specialties occur simultaneously, and a doctor who is an obstetrician/gynecologist is called an ob-gyn.

DADFINITION

An obstetrician and a gynecologist can be the same person, or different people, but you'll figure out the difference eventually because you'll visit the office no fewer than a hundred times before, during, and after pregnancy.

A pregnant woman visits her obstetrician no less than a thousand times each week and will ask you to come along. A few of the visits are fun—those that involve ultrasounds—but most of the visits take an absurd amount of time. After the baby is born, the visits will be less frequent, but those missing visits are replaced with taking the baby to the pediatrician.

Once the baby is old enough, or mom has recovered fully from labor or a C-section, you can respectfully decline accompanying your partner on visits to the doctor. You'll have to keep up with old issues of *Vanity Fair* some other way.

OVERDUE PREGNANCY

DEFINITION

Technically, an overdue pregnancy is a pregnancy that goes two weeks past a woman's estimated delivery date, or EDD. However, today, "overdue pregnancy" is the term commonly used to describe a pregnancy that goes even a day beyond an EDD.

Women who go more than a week past their due date—and their babies—are typically monitored to make sure the pregnancy is still progressing in a healthy way. Doctors are willing to let women continue healthy pregnancies past their due dates because due dates are really only an estimate of when the baby will be delivered. However, if a woman goes too far past her due date, the doctor may recommend inducing labor.

DADFINITION

An overdue pregnancy is overtime in a game that eventually has to end. There will be a winner. Hopefully it doesn't go into a sudden death shootout because there's so much pressure!

Seriously though, if your partner is overdue, get ready to spend some time with an anxious, cranky pregnant woman. At this point, she's probably done being pregnant . . . and you're probably done with her being done with being pregnant. So hurry already, kid! We're dying out here!

PLACENTA

DEFINITION

The placenta attaches the baby to the mother's uterus during pregnancy. It provides the baby with needed nutrients; moves waste and various gases away from the baby; and produces a variety of hormones, such as estrogen and progesterone, that prepare the mother's body for the various stages of pregnancy and labor.

The placenta is typically expelled about fifteen to twenty minutes after the birth of the child, and since the placenta can cause health risks if not removed, the doctor will have to make sure it comes out . . . one way or another.

DADFINITION

Consider the placenta to be an important part of pregnancy, only it shows up after labor like an unwelcome party guest . . . one that brings an integral part of the main course. Yup, that's right. Some people actually eat the placenta. They cook it up and eat it like it's a twenty-ounce rib-eye steak.

The placenta is loaded with vitamins B_6 and B_{12}, iron, estrogen, progesterone, and a few other nutrients that can help combat postpartum depression. The placenta is also packed with minerals, oxygen, and nutrients; is supposedly great for mom; and can be made into smoothies or replace the meat in any common meal. If this is your thing, that's all well and good, but if it's not, feel free to thaw those frozen meals that your partner made in bulk while she was nesting and breathe a sigh of relief.

PUSH PRESENT

DEFINITION

A push present is a gift given to a new mom (usually by a new dad) to mark the occasion of her delivering a baby. Also known as a push gift or baby bauble, a push present is pretty much a way for the dad (or even the mom's parents, relatives, or friends) to thank the mom for all the work she did during pregnancy and labor and delivery. The present may be given before, or after, the child's birth and in some instances has even been given in the delivery room.

DADFINITION

A push present is given to a mother after the birth of her child when having a child isn't enough of a gift. "Congratulations on the birth of your child, which is cool and all, but if your pink and screaming kid isn't really doing it for you, here's an expensive watch."

Push presents became popular once celebrities began to get them after they had a child . . . probably to soften the blow that they're most likely birthing another person who hates their guts.

In my opinion, push presents are allowed as long as your friends, relatives, or baby mama don't guilt you into buying one. A genuine gift from the heart isn't the worst idea in the world for the woman who just pushed out a baby. When you're making the purchase, think small, sentimental, and special. Maybe something from the expensive rows of snacks in the hospital vending machine.

STRETCH MARKS

DEFINITION

Stretch marks are pink, red, or purple indented streaks that appear on skin that has been stretched. They commonly appear on the thighs, breasts, and abdomen on a pregnant women during the late second trimester throughout the third trimester. While stretch marks start out pink, purple, or red in color, they typically fade to white or gray over time. While treatment can help stretch marks fade, it won't completely remove them.

DADFINITION

Stretch marks are the wounds suffered by a pregnant woman in the body's war against a child trapped inside.

You'll probably hear a great deal about stretch marks in the months after childbirth. It will be your partner's second favorite topic after losing all the baby weight. Some women don't care, or notice to care, about stretch marks, while others treat the marks with lotions, ointments, and prayers in the hope that the marks will fade over time. There are special treatments sold specifically to women worried about permanent stretch marks, but whether they actually work or not is up for debate.

SYMPATHETIC PREGNANCY

DEFINITION

Sympathetic pregnancy, also referred to as couvade syndrome, is a condition in which the male experiences many of the same symptoms and behaviors of an expectant mother.

These symptoms usually include weight gain, altered hormone levels, nausea, and altered sleep patterns. In extreme cases, symptoms can include believed labor pains, postpartum depression, and nosebleeds. The labor pain is commonly referred to as sympathy pain.

Couvade syndrome is not a recognized medical condition. Some experts feel that it's a psychosomatic condition, while others conclude it could be a biological issue linked to hormone changes.

DADFINITION

Sympathetic pregnancy could all be in a guy's head, or it could be 100-percent legit. I'm not going to make the call either way because I'm not a doctor even if I pretended to be studying to be one in college.

All I know is this: There were times in the pregnancy when I felt bad for the pain and discomfort my partner was in and thought I felt the same symptoms. There have

FICTIONAL BUT FUNNY

BAT IN THE CAVE

Another way of saying a woman is with child, the origins of "bat in the cave" are unknown, but I'll assume it was an underground swell created by DC Comics to subliminally promote the Batman movie franchise. Either that, or men are juveniles, and can't just say "my partner is pregnant" without mentioning superheroes.

also been times when I felt pain and discomfort oddly similar to the symptoms of sickness in my kids.

It's not much different than when you lie to your boss about being sick to get the day off only to actually feel sick because you sold the lie so well. The mind is a powerful thing, and if it wants to tell you that you're feeling nausea or a craving for cheese-covered fries dipped in brown gray because of your pregnant partner, it's going to do it and you're powerless to stop it.

You're also powerless against those fries. We are all powerless against those fries, my friend.

TRIAGE

DEFINITION

After hospital admission, an expectant mother is sent to the maternity triage area. The triage is the predelivery area where nurses monitor vitals and assess whether a delivery is imminent.

The nurses in the maternity triage will check a woman's temperature, urine, blood pressure, weight, body mass index (BMI), and pulse to assess the progress of the labor. They'll also ask questions regarding contractions, if any problems or issues are coming up that are associated with the labor, and general health questions to assess how far along the woman is and how soon delivery will happen.

The nurses will also go over the next steps in the birthing process, ask about birthing plans and family arrangements, and answer any questions mom or dad may have prior to the delivery.

DADFINITION

The triage is the area where a pregnant woman waits to be sent into her hospital room, and eventually the delivery room. It's the on-deck circle of the delivery.

It will also be the time that your partner will be the most panicked, so ignore your own panic for the moment and focus on her. She's been thinking about this moment for nine months, and she'll be nervous, excited, scared, and obviously incredibly uncomfortable because, oh yeah, she's about to squeeze a kid out of her vagina. It's your responsibility to keep her calm.

Your pregnant partner might also say some things she really doesn't mean due to the overwhelming feelings of the moment. A nurse asked my wife if we planned on having any more kids and before I could say,

"No, we've decided two is enough," my wife blurted out, "Maybe we'll try for a third."

The nurse was nice enough to check my vitals after I passed out.

TRIMESTERS

DEFINITION

A full-term pregnancy lasts around 40 weeks. The weeks are broken down into three equal sections, called trimesters, and each is marked by changes in the body of a pregnant woman.

The first trimester (week 1–week 12) involves the most changes in a woman's body and internal systems. Hormonal changes affect the body and cause ailments such as extreme tiredness, morning sickness, mood swings, cravings, and heartburn.

The second trimester (week 13–week 28) is slightly easier—according to most pregnant women—and symptoms such as fatigue and nausea start to subside. This trimester involves the most significant body changes and the pains that go with them, such as back and abdomen pain.

The third trimester (week 29–week 40) includes the same discomforts as those experienced in the first trimester, but most women also experience difficulty breathing because of the extra weight of the baby pressing against the lungs. They also experience frequent trips to the bathroom because the child puts pressure on the bladder, among a variety of other organs.

DADFINITION

The three trimesters are a pregnancy journey that you'll take alongside your partner. Much as your partner will experience changes, there will also be changes in you.

In the first trimester, you'll experience significant pain in your head because your partner is a sudden pain in your ass. It's not her fault—the kid is screwing with her hormones—but when she's not complaining about being sick and tired, she's usually just sick and tired.

In the second trimester things get a little better for the both of you as your partner learns to live with the sudden expansion of her body and you realize this can only last nine months and liken the whole experience to a short stint in prison. You're in prison and your cellmate can't stop eating garlic pickles.

By the third trimester you're both ready for the kid to get the hell out of her stomach. Congrats! You and the kid are both getting paroled!

ULTRASOUND

DEFINITION

An ultrasound is a type of imaging that uses a high-frequency sound wave to create an image of the inside of the womb or other body part. The sound waves reflect off internal body structures and transfer back to the ultrasound machine where they are turned into pictures called sonograms.

Ultrasound can tell expectant parents and doctors several things about the unborn baby, including the size of the baby; how well the baby's heart is working; the health of other internal organs like the spine, brain, and kidneys; and the due date of the baby, which is determined by physical growth.

Ultrasound imagery is offered to most women who are between 10–13 weeks pregnant, but can be done sooner under doctor's orders.

DADFINITION

An ultrasound is the test given to most expectant parents at four different times. The first time is to make sure the baby is inside in the womb and the pregnancy test wasn't bullshit. The second ultrasound test is to ensure the baby is healthy, the third ultrasound is to find out the sex of the baby, and the final ultrasound is to estimate when the hell the kid is going to come firing out.

The result of the ultrasound, the sonogram, is a picture that can be used to announce you're pregnant or to give other family members heart attacks. I suggest finding a special way to announce the pregnancy such as putting the sonogram inside your mother's birthday card, having it printed onto coffee mugs for the office, or scanning it and posting to Facebook to let everyone know your life of leisure and freedom will come to an end in roughly nine months.

Feel free to keep your kid's ultrasound and use it to occasionally scare the crap out of relatives because it's fun.

UMBILICAL CORD

DEFINITION

The umbilical cord (also called the navel string or birth cord) is a conduit between the developing embryo or fetus and the placenta.

The umbilical cord is attached to the baby on one end through an opening in the baby's abdomen, and to the placenta, which is attached to the uterine wall, on the other end. The placenta provides the baby with needed nutrients; moves waste and various gases away from the baby; and produces a variety of hormones, such as estrogen and progesterone that prepare the mother's body for the various stages of pregnancy and labor.

After a baby is born, the umbilical cord is clamped off and cut close to the baby's abdomen, leaving an umbilical stump and, later, a bellybutton.

DADFINITION

The umbilical cord is the original lifeline.

It's also the first test to see if you've got the stomach to be a dad. In the delivery room, the nurse will ask if you'd like to cut the cord. You can say yes, step on up, and use a massive set of shears to snip a cord attached to both your partner and your new child.

You could abstain and say, "Nah, I'm cool," then try and keep your vending-machine-bought sandwich from coming back up and getting dumped onto your scrub-covered feet.

So, yes, the umbilical cord is a lifeline, but you may want to phone a friend to get him to come down and cut the cord because there's a good chance your stomach will be in knots.

UMBILICAL STUMP

DEFINITION

The umbilical stump is the part of the umbilical cord that remains attached to the newborn after birth. Once the baby is born, the umbilical stump is clamped and, a week or so after birth, will shrivel up, turn black, and drop off. There will be a small wound left behind. When that wound heals, it will become the baby's bellybutton.

The baby's umbilical stump must be kept clean to prevent infection. During bath time, use a sponge or washcloth to clean the area. A milk soap or baby shampoo is fine for keeping the area clean, but plain water will suffice.

DADFINITION

The umbilical stump is the dark remains left over after cutting the umbilical cord. It will freak you out for weeks and make you consider the purpose of the bellybutton.

Until the stump falls off, you'll stare at it, poke at it, let it gross you out, and reimagine the moment you or the nurse snipped the umbilical cord to detach your kid from her mom. It will creep you out. It might even turn your stomach. But don't worry, this is natural. Childbirth is an awesome and gross experience, but you tend to forget how disgusting because it's so monumental.

The cord, and eventually the bellybutton, will make you analyze your own belly button. Then you'll stare at it, poke at it, prod it, and let it gross you out because you probably haven't cleaned it out in decades. You're just as disgusting as childbirth, dude, but definitely not as awesome.

VERNIX

DEFINITION

Vernix, also known as vernix caseosa, is the white, waxy coating that develops on the skin of a fetus inside the womb.

The level of vernix on a child declines over the course of the pregnancy. Full-term babies are typically born without much vernix coating their skin, while premature infants have a thicker layer of the white, waxy substance.

Nurses usually remove vernix shortly after birth by wiping and bathing the baby. In the past few years, mothers have requested leaving the child coated in vernix because of its health benefits, such as being a natural moisturizer for a newborn's skin, and due to fears of the possible chemicals used when bathing a seconds-old infant.

DADFINITION

Vernix is the waxy substance on a newborn's skin that makes your newborn look like an extra in a horror movie or a future grand champion in Olympic Slip 'N Slide.

Whether your child is wiped down and/or bathed after birth or remains coated in what looks like cottage cheese before being handed over to his happy and exhausted parents doesn't really matter. You won't notice anyway. Half of your mind will be occupied with the sheer magnitude of the moment while the other half of your mind will scream, *"Don't drop the kid!"* which is almost like mentally screaming, *"Drop the kid!"* Does it ever work when you mentally scream, *"Don't miss this putt!"* at yourself? Why should holding a kid be different? Just relax.

Let the half-euphoric/half-panicked moment wash over you because you'll never be this happy and scared in your life ever again. Until you have another kid.

WATER BIRTH

DEFINITION

A water birth is a birth that takes place in water (bathtub, low-temperature hot tub, or any other water-filled basin) either in a hospital, at home, or in a birthing center.

If a water birth is performed at a hospital, the pregnant woman and baby will receive the same standard of care used for another type of labor and delivery. Hospitals that have been set up to accommodate this course of action will have a special underwater fetal heartbeat monitor to make sure the baby isn't distressed.

During a water birth, a pregnant woman can labor *and* deliver in the water or move out of the water for the actual delivery. If the woman delivers in the water, the midwife or nurse will immediately remove the baby from the tub and perform the usual health checks done on a newborn.

DADFINITION

A water birth gives dads all the excitement of being at the pool on a warm summer day, except your partner is giving birth and everyone is staring.

So is a water birth worth it? The results are actually mixed. Some studies say a water birth is great with a bunch of benefits. Some say there's no difference between a water birth and any other type of birth. Some believe a water birth offers laboring moms a natural, soothing environment for delivery. Other people feel it's like the worst ride at the water park.

If you opt for a water birth in the home, be prepared for a large amount of water to get all over the floor, and to never be able to walk into your living room again without thinking about what went on in there.

WOMB

DEFINITION

The womb, another term for the uterus, is the part of the female reproductive system that holds a developing baby during pregnancy.

Throughout the woman's pregnancy, the womb changes to accommodate the needs of the ever-growing baby. It actually grows from the size of a fist to roughly the size of a watermelon when the baby is full term. During labor and delivery, the muscles in the womb shorten and contract to help move the baby out of the body.

DADFINITION

The womb is the protective area inside the mom where the baby gets to hang out for nine months. After she is born, she'll spend the next seventy or more years of her life trying to get back in because life was much easier on the inside than it is on the outside.

With every sonogram printout during our two pregnancies, I liked to imagine our unborn babies acting inside the womb much like the fetus in the early scenes in the movie *Look Who's Talking*. The child discovers his hands and feet for the first time, does backflips, and passes the time making adult observations (from his still developing brain). I also like to imagine people remember the movie *Look Who's Talking* . . .

ZYGOTE

DEFINITION

A zygote is the one-celled organism that is created when the sperm fertilizes an egg.

Over the next two weeks, known as the germinal period of development, the zygote's cell and then cells divide through mitosis, a process where each cell divides into two cells and so on and so forth. The zygote eventually becomes an embryo and implants in the uterus.

DADFINITION

A zygote is the product of a fertilized egg. You're the fertilizer of that egg. Congratulations, your childhood dreams of being a farmer have been realized.

Fertilization, which is kind of like the female egg and male sperm having sex on their own, is the first step in a complex series of events that leads to the baby bump. When the egg and sperm unite, they form the single-celled zygote.

"Zygote" will be the most "science" you'll have to learn as a new dad. I promise. That said, I can't make any guarantees about what will happen when your former zygote reaches high school and learns about zygotes, embryos, and human reproduction. You're on your own at that point.

PART 2

THE FIRST YEAR

Ask any parents who are this far into the game and they'll say the first year is the most challenging . . . which is a nice way to put it.

Those same parents will also agree that the first year is also full of some amazing milestones. Even though it feels like a large chunk of time is spent feeding and changing diapers, and you'll wonder how one kid can produce so much poo, it's a time when your newborn begins to develop into an individual. You'll miss this year, if not the lack of sleep, once it has passed, especially when your once one-year-old reaches the teen years and finds other, more frightening ways to keep you up at night.

In this section of the book, you'll learn all you need to know about the words, terms, and phrases that spring up most often when caring for, and chasing around, your child in his or her first year of life.

ALOPECIA

DEFINITION

Alopecia, medically known as alopecia areata, is hair loss that occurs when the immune system attacks hair follicles as a way to protect the body from illness. The hair follicles begin to shrink and produce hair at a much slower rate. This hair loss can affect adults and children.

There is no cause for alarm since alopecia areata isn't painful. It also doesn't mean that the child is unhealthy. It is actually common for infants to lose patches of hair in the first four to six months of life, even if they were born with a thick head of hair, and some kids don't have hair for almost the first year of life. Even if a child loses her hair in infancy, it's not always directly associated with alopecia. In most cases, a child losing the hair from birth is natural.

DADFINITION

Alopecia in children is when your baby is barely out of the womb and already sporting your slowly balding dome. Luckily for the kid, alopecia is a pretty common affliction for little ones. The alopecia is most likely genetic, though it might not be your fault—one in five kids who have the disorder also have a family member who suffers from the ailment. Unlike your suddenly shining dome, the child's hair will grow back.

Besides alopecia, a bald patch along the back of the head can also occur due to the baby rubbing her scalp against the mattress during sleep. Again, the hair will grow back. And, if you're really self-conscious about the bald head, try caps or other headwear.

I meant for you, not the kid.

APGAR SCORE

DEFINITION

The Apgar score is a numerical summary of a newborn's condition at birth.

Developed more than fifty years ago by an anesthesiologist named Virginia Apgar, Apgar is also an acronym for Appearance, Pulse, Grimace response, Activity, and Respiration. Each section is ranked on a scale of 0–2 with a "perfect" overall score being a 10.

The Apgar score is calculated in the delivery room right after the baby's birth, then again at five minutes after birth. The test was designed to evaluate the physical condition of a newborn and gauge if there's an immediate need for extra medical or emergency care.

DADFINITION

Consider the Apgar test your baby's first test. The kid has been on planet Earth for mere seconds and she's already being tested and evaluated. Hopefully she's brought along a couple of sharpened number two pencils.

It's vital to put this score in perspective. The test's main function is to quickly assess the overall condition of the newborn. It's a way to decipher if the baby needs immediate medical attention. You want to keep in mind that the Apgar score doesn't predict a baby's long-term health, behavior, intellect, personality, or outcome. In most cases, a perfectly healthy newborn sometimes scores low because of the method of birth—vaginal delivery or cesarean—and very few babies score a perfect 10.

Don't stress over the test. You'll have plenty of other tests to stress over in the coming days and months.

BABBLING

DEFINITION

Babbling is a prelinguistic skill that happens in infants prior to the development of language and speech. There are three types of babbling in infants, and they occur at different times in the child's development.

- Marginal babbling occurs between four and six months of age and refers to the sounds a child makes when putting together a consonant and a vowel for monosyllabic sounds.
- Reduplicated babbling refers to an infant repeating the same syllable over and over, like "ma ma ma ma."
- In the final stage of babbling, known as nonreduplicated babbling, the sounds become more varied and the child will put together consonants and vowels in an attempt to make actual words or repeat words said to them in conversation.

DADFINITION

Babbling is an activity that may get on your nerves because it is never-ending. That said, you should respond back in a similar sound to encourage your child to continue. This helps boost both the receptive language (where he understands the words that he hears) and expressive language (where he becomes capable of saying those words back), which are both crucial if you hope to actually have a real conversation one day.

So encourage the babbling. Your infant is probably the only person in the house listening to what you're saying anyway. You might as well take advantage.

BABY BLUES

DEFINITION

Most new moms experience what is known as the "baby blues," which is categorized by sudden mood swings, crying jags, bouts of lethargy, feelings of inadequacy as a mother and as a person, and an overall feeling of anxiety. Typically the baby blues begin about three to four days after delivery and last about two weeks. Between 60–80 percent of moms experience the baby blues.

If the baby blues last longer than a week, and a severe attitude change persists, the baby blues may turn into a case of postpartum depression, a disorder categorized by insomnia, severe mood swings, and the inability to bond with the baby. For most women, the depression eventually subsides in a few months; however, some mothers suffer for much longer and can fall into a deep depression.

DADFINITION

Just when you think your partner's hormones should start settling down, in come the baby blues!

As the father of a new child, and the husband to a new mother, it's crucial to pay very close attention to the feelings, temperament, and mood swings of your partner. The baby blues are mostly caused by lack of sleep, changing hormones, and the stress and anxiety brought on by the responsibility of caring for a newborn.

Oddly, fathers can also suffer from the baby blues. After my first child, I had a strong case of the baby blues that felt as though they lasted much longer than a few weeks. Eventually, once I was getting a little more sleep at night, and life returned to as close to normal as it could get, the feelings of depression and lethargy subsided. With my second born, I had absolutely no signs of the baby blues, most likely because I knew exactly what to expect with a new child.

Note: If any of the warning signs for postpartum depression are present, in either you or your spouse, talk to a professional as soon as possible. In most cases, it's just a case of the baby blues, but if your partner is acting different than normal, especially towards the baby, you want to seek assistance from a person specializing in postpartum depression cases.

BABY LOTION

DEFINITION

Baby lotion is a lotion that is specially formulated to be gentle on very young skin. It is rubbed on the baby's skin to keep it soft after baths and in the harsh winter months.

Most baby lotions are essentially a blend of oil and water designed to cleanse, moisturize, and protect the baby's skin. Baby lotion can be used as an alternative to baby wipes by wiping away with a dry cloth and then a cloth with lotion to prevent chafing. If the child suffers from very sensitive skin, there are a number of fragrance-free options on the market. However, if the baby's skin becomes irritated—either from baby lotion use or other reasons—you should seek the advice of your doctor, health advisor, or other healthcare professional.

DADFINITION

Baby lotion is just one of the many products needed to keep the baby happy—too bad you'll forget to apply it every time.

Much like adults, children have hygiene routines. Parents are expected to remember these routines along with the hundred other steps in caring for a child. Sometimes things get forgotten like lotion after a bath or a bottle after a nap or a diaper change after one or seven hours. People forget!

Baby lotion is also perfect for keeping your skin moisturized and to prevent you from smelling like a Times Square derelict after you've forgotten to shower for a couple of days. Perfect for baby, perfect for you. A win-win!

BABYWEARING

DEFINITION

Babywearing is carrying a baby in a soft carrier, either a sling, pouch, or wrap. Babywearing is more convenient for new parents because it frees the hands to complete other activities while allowing the mother to still be close to the baby.

Babywearing has been a popular practice around the world for centuries, but Dr. William Sears and his wife, Martha, advocates of attachment parenting, coined the actual term a few decades ago.

Advocates claim that babywearing results in children who cry less, form a stronger bond with parents, and tend to be more organized and intelligent later in life due to the added stimulation and interaction.

DADFINITION

Babywearing is the act of turning a child into a backpack. Only this backpack cries, craps, and occasionally takes blows to the face when mom or dad doesn't take clearance space into consideration.

Babywearing is beneficial for new moms who want to get stuff done around the house while still holding their child as much as possible, which is great! The trouble comes in when you consider the fact another human is constantly, and literally, attached at the hip. It also makes it harder for you or mom to put the child down because the child isn't accustomed to being so far away from a parent.

Be careful. A slingy baby could develop into a clingy baby, and it's much harder to carry a teenager on your back.

BASSINET

DEFINITION

A bassinet, or cradle, is a bed specifically made for babies to sleep in from birth to about four months of age. Once the baby is old enough to roll himself over, he should be moved to a proper crib.

Most bassinets are designed to rock or swing freely as a way to calm crying or restless newborns. The swinging or rocking process is called lulling a child to sleep.

A bassinet is usually placed at the foot of the parent's bed or in the bedroom so that nursing mothers can have quicker access to newborns for nighttime feeding.

DADFINITION

Bassinets are beds for the world's most unpredictable alarm clock.

A bassinet is for sleeping and is not to be confused with the medieval war helmet called the bascinet. However, every bassinet should come with a bascinet because you'll wish for a metal war helmet to cover your head and muffle the sounds of your screaming baby.

Speaking of war gear, bassinets are a double-edged sword. On one hand, it's helpful to have the newborn so close for nighttime feedings so you can quickly retrieve her to muffle early morning wails, but on the other hand, the child is sleeping in the same room so say goodbye to watching TV in bed, farting too loud, or having any type of sexual relations.

It's also hard to fake not hearing the baby cry when she's a foot away and wailing as frequently as police sirens in the worst part of town.

BREAST ABSCESS

DEFINITION

A breast abscess is the result of an uncomfortable infection (called mastitis) and inflammation of the tissue around the breast. A breast abscess is usually the result of an infection of an untreated crack of the skin around the nipple that occurs if bacteria enter the breast tissue during breastfeeding. Infections can also occur if the milk ducts become blocked.

If a new mother has a breast abscess, the abscess might need to be drained, which is done using a needle and syringe. For larger and more troublesome abscesses, a small incision may be necessary to drain the pus from the infected area.

DADFINITION

A breast abscess is one of the many issues that comes after the birth of your child that you can do little to prevent or even help soothe. Sorry dads! That said, even if you can't help solve the problem, it's important for you to know that your partner will likely suffer from any number of issues that will, along with the care of the newborn, cause her to feel a little worse than usual.

While you can do nothing about the uncomfortableness or overall suckiness of breast abscesses, you can be on the lookout for other medical issues that could be directly linked to an untreated breast abscess and widespread infection such as sudden confusion or loss of consciousness, difficulty breathing, decrease in urine, fainting, or high fever. Get prompt medical care for your partner if any of those symptoms occur.

BREASTFEEDING

DEFINITION

Breastfeeding is the act of feeding an infant using the milk created in the breast of the mother.

The American Academy of Pediatrics recommends that babies be breastfed for "1 year or longer as mutually desired by mother and infant," and that babies be breastfed exclusively for the first six months because it's the best way to provide nutrition for an infant. Breast milk contains enzymes that assist with digestion, as well as vital nutrients like proteins, vitamins, carbohydrates, and fats that are important for the child's health. Breast milk also bolsters immunity and helps infants resist infection.

DADFINITION

Ah, breastfeeding. The only thing that will keep you in bed during a 2 A.M. feeding! But while breastfeeding might be easier for you, it's actually a, if not *the*, major hot-button topic of pregnancy and motherhood. The research and results showing the benefits of breastfeeding are everywhere, but that doesn't mean it's the best course of action for mom.

Your partner will feel pressure from both of the breastfeeding camps, but it's still strictly her call. Your only course of action is to make your opinions known but support whichever side she chooses. After all, it's still her body, even if another human life is counting on it for food. And it's not as though the child will starve or fail on formula alone. So support your partner in whatever she decides, even if that means you'll have to drag yourself out of bed for that early morning feeding . . .

BREAST PUMP

DEFINITION

A breast pump is a device that uses suction to pull milk from the breasts. There are manually and electrically operated breast pumps. Though significantly more expensive, electric pumps are far easier to use and more likely to maintain the flow of milk.

Women use breast pumps for a variety of reasons: to feed babies who aren't able to latch onto the breast, to store milk for later use, or to encourage milk production.

DADFINITION

A breast pump is an outrageously noisy device that looks like an air horn. You'll want to pick it up, make a fake horn sound, and cheer on your favorite sports team.

Breast pumps will be your best friend and your worst nightmare. On one hand, the pumps help deliver the key to keeping your baby healthy, happy, and quiet—the invaluable boob juice. On the other hand, even if the baby isn't hungry or if breast milk is in plentiful supply, your partner will have to do what's known as the pump and dump. The pump and dump is not a former professional wrestling tag team, it's the process of pumping out breast milk and throwing it away because it's not needed.

If your partner uses a breast pump, she's likely going to have the air horn attached to her breast for at least the first few months after the baby arrives, and it's not the most comfortable process, so try to keep the pump-and-dump puns to a minimum, no matter how funny they sound in your head.

BURPING

DEFINITION

Burping is the release of gas from the digestive tract through the mouth. Burping is incredibly important to aid in the comfort and digestion of a newborn.

Both formula-fed and breastfed babies need to be burped during and after feedings. However, formula-fed babies need to be burped more frequently. This is due to the excess air that these babies ingest due to the fast flow of the formula from the bottle. Breastfed babies are able to better regulate the milk flow, which means they ingest less air.

DADFINITION

Burping is something that feels just as good for a kid as it does for an adult.

A massive belch from your kid feels like a job well done for both him, for letting one rip, and you, for helping him get all of the gas out. The louder the prouder.

There are a couple of things to keep in mind when you burp an infant. You probably know that you need to pat him on the back, but you should also make sure he sits upright, and you should put some pressure on his belly while you pat (pound) on his back. This helps the gas leave the body easily. If your baby is especially gassy, there are also a few over-the-counter products available that can help him out. Just place a few drops right into the bottle at feeding time to make the nursery sound less like a frat house.

CHILDPROOFING

DEFINITION

Childproofing (also referred to as babyproofing) is the act of making an environment—usually the home—safer for young children.

Childproofing involves the removal of both the obvious and hidden dangers that are easily within reach of crawling or walking children. There are several areas of danger to consider once the child is around and mobile, including the child's access to electrical outlets, toxic chemicals, medications and medical supplies, tools, and even the toys of older siblings.

Childproofing can also entail the blockage of access to certain areas of the house through the use of baby gates, fences, and portable playpens.

DADFINITION

Childproofing is something that you do to keep your child safe, even though it basically makes living in your house much more difficult. Want to go into your kitchen? Good luck opening that baby gate! Want to access your cleaning supplies? Not if those baby locks have anything to say about it!

So why do it? Well, experts claim that kids between the ages of one and four are two times as likely to be killed by choking, chemical burns, drowning, fire, poisoning, or falls around the home than by the violence of a stranger. Congratulations on learning one more nugget of fact to keep you up at night! The good thing is that childproofing the house is a pretty simple task. The first, and probably simplest, step is to think like a kid. Crawl on the floor, look around, and think, "What would I jam down my throat if I were a kid?" Another idea is to just let the kid roam, staying one step behind, and let the kid show you everything she'll grab off a shelf or stick up her nose.

I'm sorry to let you know that childproofing is a never-ending process, and as the child grows, so do all the hidden dangers within reach. Just pack up everything and hide it until she's a teen.

CIRCUMCISION

DEFINITION

Circumcision is the medical procedure of removing the foreskin from the head of the penis, exposing the tip.

Circumcision is typically performed on male newborns or young children, and is typically done during the first ten days of life—often within the first forty-eight hours—either in the hospital or in the home during a religious service.

Approximately 55–65 percent of all newborn boys in the United States are circumcised each year, though the rate varies by region. The procedure of circumcision is much more common in the United States, Canada, and the Middle East and not as common in South and Central America and throughout most of Europe.

DADFINITION

Circumcision. The term that makes all grown men shudder. That said, congratulations on making it this far in the book without passing out or turning to the next entry with sympathy pains.

For some parents, the choice to circumcise a child is a relatively easy decision. In fact, it might not even be a decision at all but more of a foregone conclusion because of cultural or religious beliefs. For others, to circumcise or not is a medical decision made after research is completed and the pros and cons of having the procedure done are weighed.

Circumcision does carry potential risks, just like any surgical procedure, so it's wise to decide before the birth of the child either against or for skin. See what I did there? For skin. Foreskin. Sorry, couldn't resist.

CLOTH DIAPERS

DEFINITION

A cloth diaper is a reusable diaper made from manmade materials and natural fibers. The natural fibers can be cotton, wool, bamboo, or unbleached hemp. The manmade materials are usually an absorbent layer of microfiber to prevent leaking.

Modern cloth diapers come in several different shapes and forms with nine common types:

- **Flats:** large squares of single-layer fabric usually made of cotton
- **Prefolds:** rectangular pieces of cloth folded into sections with the middle portion being the most absorbent layer
- **Fitted:** usually made of cotton, bamboo, hemp, or fleece and usually super absorbent compared to other cloth diapers
- **Contours:** a combination of prefolds and fitted but require pins to stay in place and a cover to keep clothes from getting wet
- **Hybrids:** a combination of cloth and disposable diapers
- **Pockets:** the modern cloth diaper, each diaper includes a pocket that must be stuffed with an absorbent insert made from the popular cloth diaper materials
- **Sleeve diapers:** similar to pocket diapers except these cloth diapers have two pockets, in front and in back, that need stuffing
- **All-in-two:** similar to pocket diapers except an insert is snapped inside instead of stuffing pockets
- **All-in-one:** cloth diapers that are just like disposable diapers but instead of throwing them away they're thrown in the laundry for wash and reuse

DADFINITION

Cloth diapers are just one more baby item to wash.

Mom will make the decision on diapers long before the child comes along. She'll decide either from personal preference, advice from other moms, or one of the countless articles she's read during pregnancy swayed her opinion.

Each camp—cloth diaper users versus the disposable crew—will explain why its diaper ideas make the most sense, but cloth diapers do have a distinct advantage over traditional disposable diapers just because of the amount of money spent on diapers over the course of just a few years. All of that money could have been spent on other things, like a water bill and laundry detergent, because cloth diapers need to get washed constantly.

Just practice with whichever diaper mom chooses long before the kid arrives and you'll be fine.

CLUSTER FEEDING

DEFINITION

A cluster feeding is a group of feedings closely spaced together, which is typically followed by a longer than usual time between feedings. While babies usually get hungry every 2–3 hours, during a cluster feeding they may want to eat as often as every 30–45 minutes.

Cluster feedings generally occur based on the baby and her hunger signs. She may cry and become fussy during the time of a cluster feeding. That said, babies will most often cluster feed in the evening or in the early hours of the morning.

Cluster feeding is most commonly observed among breastfed babies, but it is also seen in babies who are formula-fed.

DADFINITION

Cluster feeding is when it feels like your newborn child has been replaced with a ravenous college student scavenging the cabinets for food.

Cluster feeding isn't so bad during the day, but cluster feeding at night is a little harder to manage. Waking up every 45 minutes to eat isn't going to make you look very refreshed in the morning. Also be sure not to eat when the kid eats. Your tubby frame doesn't need anymore 3 A.M. ice cream treats.

Cluster feeding won't seem real at first. You'll think something else is wrong with your kid. "He can't possibly be hungry again," you'll say, and do everything but feed the child while he cries and cries because he's hungry as hell. Finally, you'll run out of ideas and shove a bottle in his mouth (or shove him in the arms of his mom to nurse) only to realize, "Oh, yeah, he was hungry again."

COLIC

DEFINITION

Colic is a pattern of intense and inconsolable crying that recurs around the same time every day. It usually occurs in the late afternoon and early evening and can last throughout the night. A healthy baby is diagnosed with colic when he cries for more than 3 hours a day, for more than 3 days a week, for more than 3 weeks in a row.

The cause of colic is unknown, and it typically begins in the early weeks of the child's life and can continue up to three months of age. Theories behind the causes of colic include minor stomach distress, reflux or heartburn due to stomach acid, a growing digestive system with spasming muscles, or gas.

DADFINITION

Colic is the most frustrating of all the possible conditions in a child because no one knows why it happens or what could be done to stop it.

Imagine that there's something wrong with your car. Maybe the trunk opens itself up every time you drop into neutral. Over the last week, you've lost a number of things that have fallen out of your trunk and you're at your wit's end. You bring the car into the shop, but they can't tell you what's wrong! Except, with colic, the trunk is a high-pitched, never-ending cry; what you've lost are hours of much-needed sleep; and the car is a tiny, little being who lives in your house. It's pretty intense.

The only way to put an end to a colicky kid is to try every remedy, one at a time, until the issue stops—or until your baby grows out of it. It could take days or even weeks or months, but once relief comes, it will feel just as good for you as it does for your car, er, kid.

COLOSTRUM

DEFINITION

Typically referred to as "first milk," colostrum is immature or early breast milk that is higher in protein, carbohydrates, and antibodies, and lower in fat than breast milk produced later in the breastfeeding process. This special milk is yellowish orange in color and thick and sticky.

Colostrum is easily digestible and acts as a laxative. This is important because expelling waste helps a newborn excrete excess bilirubin, a waste product of red blood cells, preventing jaundice. Colostrum matures into breast milk over the first couple of weeks of breastfeeding.

DADFINITION

Colostrum, no matter how much it looks like liquid earwax, is the perfect breast milk for babies. It's so perfect, I'm shocked that adults haven't started drinking colostrum in some new health craze.

Don't misunderstand—grown adults are chugging colostrum, but it's coming from the farm and not the nursery. Colostrum from cows is a popular drink of choice with adults who are lactose intolerant, and many people use bovine colostrum to boost the immune system and repair the nervous system. It's even used in hospitals to treat patients with head injuries.

It's only a matter of time before the *New York Times* runs a feature about the benefits of human colostrum in humans over the age of the average PBS Kids viewer. Next thing you know, athletes will get busted for high levels of colostrum, and *60 Minutes* will do an entire cover story on black-market colostrum sales.

People are lunatics when it comes to their kids but get even crazier when it comes to their own body. They'll eat, sip, and consume anything to get the edge and possibly live forever—no matter how bad it makes their breakfast cereal taste.

COSLEEPING

DEFINITION

Cosleeping refers to the sharing of a bed with newborns and infants instead of putting them to sleep in a bassinet or crib.

There are two camps in the cosleeping debate. Many experts and parents feel that having a "family bed" is a perfect situation that strengthens the bonds between parent and child, makes nursing easier for both mom and baby, and allows for more time for mom or dad to hold the child.

The alternative camp believes cosleeping prevents a baby from learning to fall asleep on her own, discourages the independence of a child, and often leads to sleeping issues later in life.

Cosleeping is a standard practice in many parts of the world but has only recently been used in places like Europe, North America, and Australia due to the rise in attachment parenting.

DADFINITION

"Cosleeping" is a deceptive term that assumes that when a newborn child comes back into the home there will be any sleeping at all.

Much like every single other decision in parenting, cosleeping has its cheerleaders and detractors. It's also completely up to the parents. It's best to discuss the matter before the kid arrives so you and your partner aren't verbally slugging it out at two in the morning when one parent wants the kid in the bed so everyone can get some sleep and the other doesn't want to get into the habit. It's also best to try it at least once because you really can't make an informed decision until you experience a bed full of bodies.

Cosleeping also depends on the child. Some kids take to it immediately, while others can't make it through the night because you and your partner both snore like farm animals.

CRADLE CAP

DEFINITION

"Cradle cap"—or infantile seborrheic dermatitis if you're being incredibly specific—is the term for the flakes of dry skin or the yellowish, crusty patches most often found on the top of a newborn baby's skull. While cradle cap most often occurs on the top of the head, it sometimes occurs in other areas on a child including the ears and eyebrows, eyelids, and armpits.

The exact cause of cradle cap is unknown, but experts believe that the hormones a baby receives from mom at the end of pregnancy could be the culprit.

DADFINITION

Cradle cap is dry skin on your baby that will bother you more than any type of dry skin that you've ever had in your life. The good thing is that while it isn't the most adorable thing to look at on a child, it's harmless and usually clears up on its own in about six to twelve months.

If cradle cap persists and the constant flakes really bother you, there are a few remedies that could clear it up quicker like gently massaging the child's head with your fingers or a brush or shampooing the hair a little more frequently. If all else fails, there are specific shampoos for cradle cap and even natural oils that can be applied.

It's not caused by poor hygiene or allergies, and it's not contagious and doesn't seem to bother newborns at all (no matter how much it might drive you nuts).

DEMAND FEEDING

DEFINITION

Demand feeding means feeding your baby whenever she presents hunger cues, such as rooting, crying, or chewing on her hands, that let you know she wants to eat. Demand feeding is the opposite of scheduled feeding where an infant is fed on a set schedule.

DADFINITION

Demand feeding is the idea of feeding your little dictator whenever she snaps her fingers and tells you that she must eat now! Since, when you demand feed, you're basically at the whim of a tiny tyrant, it's important to learn the difference between hunger signals and other signals a newborn may give.

Though they can't speak, newborns tend to give off a certain cry depending on what they want. There is an "I'm hungry" cry, an "I'm tired" cry, an "I want my mom" cry, and a "Hmm, this house seems too quiet right now" cry. You'll learn to decipher each cry and react accordingly.

When in doubt, and the crying won't stop, shove a bottle in her mouth.

DIAPER BAG

DEFINITION

A diaper bag is a bag that contains the essentials you need to care for your baby but also incidental items like an extra pair of clothes, sunscreen, toys, snacks, and a changing pad.

Diaper bags come in different shapes and sizes but are generally small enough to fit on or under a stroller. Some bags can be larger if carrying accessories for more than one child.

DADFINITION

A diaper bag is a carryall for moms to store everything a baby and a traveling mom would need on their short trip. Also inside the bag are anything a baby and a traveling mom would need if they decide to disappear forever and become gypsies or scale Mount Everest.

Moms pack diaper bags to prepare for a child-led apocalypse, while dads prefer to carry a satchel of their own that contains only a diaper, a couple of wipes, hand gel, and the map to find all of those things in case you ever forget to grab the diaper bag that was packed by your partner.

If you're out in public and must quickly retrieve an item from her diaper bag, it's best to just dump out all the contents on the floor instead of wasting time attempting to find a pacifier or bib in the endless abyss.

DIAPER RASH

DEFINITION

Diaper rash is a common irritation of a baby's skin in the areas of the body that are typically covered by a diaper, including the buttocks, genitals, lower abdomen, around the anus, and in the folds of skin in the groin.

Diaper rash can be caused by any type of an irritant that has had prolonged contact with your baby's skin. Pee and poop are both common causes of diaper rash if a diaper is left on too long. Allergies or sensitivities to the chemicals in disposable diapers, plastic pants, lotions, detergents, fabric softeners, and various powders can also cause diaper rash.

Diaper rash is less common in breastfed children and frequently occurs in kids who are eating solid foods or who have occasional bouts of diarrhea.

DADFINITION

Diaper rash is an irritation that looks more painful than it actually is. I'm just assuming this because I'm not a baby and haven't had diaper rash since forever, but it doesn't seem to be a big deal for most babies anyway.

Most rashes or marks on a child will fade over time, and you can prevent diaper rash by not letting your child sit in a wet or soiled diaper for too long. Here's a good tip that will help you keep track of the last time you've changed the baby's diaper. Just ask yourself, "When was the last time I changed his diaper?" If the answer doesn't spring immediately to mind, it's probably time to grab the diaper cream.

ECZEMA

DEFINITION

Eczema (also called atopic dermatitis) is a condition that causes itchy, inflamed skin. The resulting rash might be made up of many red, small bumps, or the condition may present itself as very dry, scaly skin.

Eczema is usually diagnosed on kids younger than five years of age. Before the age of one, babies usually develop eczema on their scalp and face. After the age of one, children are most likely to develop this rash on the insides of the elbows, the backs of the knees, the wrists, and the ankles.

DADFINITION

Eczema is a scaly, bumpy, gross rash that will make your kid itch like hell.

Fortunately, eczema isn't contagious and isn't a constant problem. Kids can have flare-ups caused by any number of factors including weather, time of year, contact with irritating creams or laundry detergents, or what side of bed they got up on in the morning. Seriously, that's what it will feel like.

The goal of treatment for eczema is to relieve and prevent further itching because itching often leads to infections. Lotions and creams like hydrocortisone are recommended to keep the skin moist. And if you can't beat the itch, take comfort in the fact that most kids grow out of this rash as they grow up. And even if they don't, at least then it won't be your problem anymore.

ENGORGEMENT

DEFINITION

Engorgement is a common occurrence in mothers after pregnancy and during the first few weeks of breastfeeding. Engorgement occurs when an abundance of milk collects in the breasts, causing swelling, hardening, and pain in the breasts and around the areola. Engorgement makes it difficult for the baby to breastfeed efficiently as the hardened nipples make latching difficult and decrease the flow of milk.

There are ways to prevent engorgement, which include letting the baby finish nursing on one breast (usually for 10–12 minutes) before moving to the other. Pumping, even if the baby isn't hungry, to alleviate milk buildup and applying cold packs to the area after feeding can also be a successful tactic.

DADFINITION

Engorgement is something that seems like it would be awesome, but it isn't.

If I told you that your partner's breasts would get substantially bigger in the weeks after delivery, you'd probably reply, "And what's the bad part?" While a woman with a bigger chest is awesome, it's not so great for her.

The thing about breastfeeding is that it's natural and ridiculously beneficial for the baby, for both nutrient intake and bonding time, but it's not the most enjoyable experience for mom. Just like pregnancy, there are countless side effects, including a ton of pain to go with the joy.

Engorgement is painful, but you could always offer to do things to ease the pain. Perhaps gently rub them for her? Just don't sound too perverted in your offer. It has probably been a long time since you were allowed to rub her breasts anyway, so you might as well both get something out of it.

EXPRESSING

DEFINITION

Expressing is drawing milk from the breasts manually (by the child) or with a breast pump. The milk will later be used for feeding or just to alleviate pressure from engorgement.

There are several medical reasons to express milk. For example, the baby may have been premature and couldn't take milk straight from the breast, or the baby may have been born with an illness or have difficulty latching, which can make breastfeeding difficult. Expressing milk that will later be fed to the baby can help the child get the benefits of breast milk without the difficulty. In addition, mothers may need to be away from their babies for a period of time, whether they've returned to the workforce or are simply gone for a few hours. By expressing milk, the mother guarantees that the caregiver feeding the baby will have a supply of breast milk available as needed.

DADFINITION

Expressing is the act of making extra milk so that mom isn't stuck with a baby attached to her teat at every moment of the day.

Expressed breast milk is helpful to have available for early morning feeding when it's your turn to wake up with the baby, for nights when a third party was nice enough to agree to watch the child, or for those moments when your partner just doesn't feel like holding the kid any longer. She'll have many of those moments, though she'll feel bad for admitting it to others (maybe even you).

Just be sure all expressed breast milk is clearly marked before it's put in the fridge. For example, you may want to label or have your partner label each bottle with the date, time the milk was expressed, and big, bold words explaining, *"This isn't half-and-half you moron!"*

FERBERIZATION

DEFINITION

Ferberization, or the Ferber method, is a "baby training" technique designed to solve infant sleep problems. Developed by Dr. Richard Ferber, Ferberization involves training infants by letting them cry for a predetermined amount of time before being soothed by their parents.

The Ferber method recommends that parents create and stick to "a warm, loving bedtime routine" and then put the baby into bed while awake, but sleepy, which teaches the child to fall asleep on his own. Parents are then instructed to use "progressive waiting" to sleep-train. In this method, the parents leave the child alone for progressively longer periods of time, even if he cries. After the predetermined amount of time has passed, parents are instructed to comfort but not to pick up or feed the infant.

The Ferber method is targeted at infants as young as four months of age and is an offshoot of the "crying it out" method, which allows kids to cry until they calm themselves down and eventually fall asleep. Often criticized by pediatricians and childcare experts, the Ferber method does have countless proponents.

DADFINITION

Ferberization is a self-soothing technique, even though it sounds like something they'd try to sell you at the auto dealer. "Do you want to winterize your car? No? Okay, do you want to Ferberize it?"

This method of sleep training is dubbed the cry-it-out method for two reasons: (1) The kid cries his face off in the crib until he falls asleep and (2) the parents cry until the kid falls asleep and worry they're doing something to damage their kid.

The Ferber method is almost as tough on parents as it is on crying children. Make sure you're both ready before implementing at bedtime.

FINE AND GROSS MOTOR SKILLS

DEFINITION

Motor skills are learned, intentional movements made by the body when the muscles, brain, and nervous system work together. There are two types of motor skills:

- Fine motor skills are the small, delicate movements that utilize the small muscles in the fingers, toes, wrists, tongue, and lips. These movements include picking up small objects using the thumb and first finger, holding utensils and bringing them to the mouth during eating, and using a pencil or crayon.
- Gross motor skills encompass big movements that use the larger muscles in the body such as the arms, legs, torso, and feet. Gross motor skills are involved in rolling over, crawling, cruising, walking, throwing, and kicking.

Gross motor skills are likely to develop before the fine motor skills. For example, a baby is able to move her arms and fingers long before she can pick up objects off the floor. Beginning around the age of eighteen months, a child learns to use both fine and gross motor skills to accomplish tasks.

DADFINITION

Fine and gross motor skills are the movements your baby makes that, in turn, make your life easier. And here you thought gross motor skills were your amazing ability to walk and fart at the same time without missing a step.

Fine and gross motor skills develop over time, but there are several ways to encourage the process through games and toys. No exercise equipment or gym membership for the kid is required (but a membership wouldn't be a bad idea for yourself).

While your child is sitting up, unsupported, place her favorite toy just out of reach to encourage her to use her gross motor skills to retrieve the toy and her fine motor skills to return the toy to its proper location. Games like Hot Potato and toys like Play-Doh help babies develop their sense of touch and texture, and stacking rings assist in developing fine motor skills.

FINGER FOODS

DEFINITION

Finger food is any food that is meant to be eaten with the hands, in contrast to being eaten with utensils. They're basically any bite-sized pieces of food that a baby can pick up and eat by himself.

Between the ages of eight and nine months, the child will probably let parents know he's ready to feed himself by grabbing the feeding spoon or snatching food off the plate. This is an important developmental step toward independence that also teaches coordination and fine motor skills . . . plus, it's fun!

DADFINITION

Finger food is any food that your kid picks up and shoves in his mouth, especially any food you put on your plate, because *your* leftover Chinese is now *his* leftover Chinese.

While you probably want to keep your Chinese food to yourself (and who wouldn't!), this is the best time to expose the kid to new foods— especially the food on your plate—to keep your child from getting into a rut with the types of food that he will or won't eat.

Food play can get messy, but take it from an anal dad and don't be in a rush to hose down your kid. Learning to self-feed is an important, hands-on learning experience. Plus, the sooner your kid learns to feed himself, the less time you'll have to deal with complete meals ground into your dining room rug or peanut butter sandwiches stuck against the wall. And that, my friend, will be a great day.

FONTANEL

DEFINITION

A fontanel is the soft spot on a baby's head where the brain is covered by a membrane instead of the skull. Whereas the hard bone of the skull would constrict the brain, this soft spot allows the brain to grow and expand during the baby's first year.

Typically, newborns have a variety of fontanels on their heads that are found on the top, the back, and both sides of the head. These should feel firm and should curve slightly inward when pressed. Over time, the fontanels harden and turn into bone like the rest of the skull.

DADFINITION

The fontanel is the soft spot on a baby's head that every person in the world is scared to go anywhere near.

It's one of the first pieces of advice you'll hear about holding your newborn baby: "You gotta watch the head." "Be careful of the head." "Not too close to the head!" People get so nervous about that soft spot they end up not holding the kid out of fear. However, unless you plan on palming your child like a brand new Spalding basketball, you'll do just fine . . . just keep the neck supported and the kid's head away from any small doorways or shoulder-level dressers.

GAS DROPS

DEFINITION

Gas drops are a liquid medication given to babies to relieve gas and any associated pain and discomfort.

Parents often use gas drops to relieve the symptoms of gas due to bottle feeding. Gas drops, which are always given orally, may be mixed into the bottle for ease of administration.

DADFINITION

Gas drops are a product you didn't realize existed until you have a kid. Then they're on your weekly shopping list because your kid is gassier than a Taco Bell patron.

If gas drops aren't available, gripe water, an all-natural gas reliever that has been used for centuries to treat gas, is a viable second option. And, if you find that gripe water works for your baby, try it on anyone with whom you have a gripe. Slip it into your partner's water bottle, and maybe she'll take an extra turn with the baby that night. Maybe not, but it's worth a try, right?

GROWTH PERCENTILE

DEFINITION

Growth percentile is a percentage measurement that tells you how your child compares in size to other kids her age.

Whenever your baby goes into the pediatrician for a wellness visit, the pediatrician will measure your baby's height, weight, and head circumference and then enter these measurements on a growth chart to see how your child compares to other children of the same sex and age. For example, if your child receives a 75 percent for weight, it means that 75 percent of children her age and size weigh less and 25 percent of children her age and size weigh more.

The growth percentile gives both you and your pediatrician an idea of how your baby is trending for general health and can be a first indicator of any problems up the road.

DADFINITION

Growth percentile is a good indicator of how big your kid is going to grow up to be, but it's important to not get too wrapped up in numbers.

Parents often get nervous when their child doesn't measure up in one of the percentiles, but it's all just estimated measures. The true test is really in the genes. If you're a family full of small people, there's a good chance your kid is never going to be tall enough to ride scary rides. If your family has to duck in every single room, your kid is more likely to be a Sasquatch.

So don't sweat the small stuff. Just like SAT scores, no one cares about your kid's growth percentile after she hits a certain age.

INFANT FORMULA

DEFINITION

Infant formula is a manufactured food designed to feed newborns and infants under twelve months of age.

The formula is usually prepared to be given to infants in bottles, but it can be mixed into foods like oatmeal and fruit and vegetable purées. Infant formula comes in either powder form (to be mixed with water) or as a premixed liquid.

Infant formula is designed to mirror a mother's breast milk, and the most popular types of infant milk include milk-based, soy-based, lactose-free, hypoallergenic, and specialty blends based on specific child needs. However, there are significant differences in the nutrient content, taste, and digestibility of these products.

DADFINITION

Infant formula is the most expensive way to feed your child.

Seriously, the cost of formula makes gas prices seem justified, but you'll suddenly be concerned with both because you'll drive miles just to find cheaper formula. This is not an overreaction; it really does cost that much.

A piece of advice—at some point, late in the evening or during an early morning feeding, you're going to wonder, "What does this stuff taste like?" and consider taking a quick suck from the bottle. Don't. It tastes just like it smells . . . bad. Take it from a man who knows.

JAUNDICE

DEFINITION

Jaundice is a yellow hue to the skin that is caused by abnormally high levels in the body of bilirubin, a yellow-colored waste product of red blood cells.

Before birth, the placenta is responsible for removing the bilirubin from the baby's blood, but after birth, the liver takes over the job. In some cases, it takes a few weeks for the baby's liver to fully get up to speed.

If the liver can't keep up with its disposal of bilirubin, the waste product builds up in the body, turning the skin of a baby yellow.

DADFINITION

The yellow tint that jaundice gives your baby is just one of the many colors he will turn in his first few months.

There's yellow for jaundice, red for rashes, and some kids turn orange from eating too many orange-tinted foods like yams and carrots. This happened to my kids, and people thought we took them to tanning beds or got spray tans. Nope, those little buggers just love them some sweet potatoes.

Jaundice isn't fun, but it goes away eventually. In the meantime, embrace the rainbow!

KANGAROO CARE

DEFINITION

Kangaroo care is the act of a parent holding a newborn skin to skin in order to facilitate bonding between the parent and the child. The baby is dressed in a diaper and a hat and is held chest to chest with her parent. A wrap is placed around both the baby and parent for warmth and security. The baby's head is often turned to the side so that the baby can hear the heartbeat of her parent.

While kangaroo care is used with full-term babies, it is most often used with preterm babies and can help with the preemie's development.

DADFINITION

Kangaroo care is the act of holding a child skin to skin, because holding a half-naked baby never gets old.

There are few things I'll genuinely miss about having young children. People will lie and say they'll miss some stuff, but I'll remember all the hassles and it will all cancel out. What I'll really miss is holding a naked-just-before-getting-into-the-bathtub kid. There's just something about it. It's more than a bonding experience. It's almost spiritual. This is my kid and this is me, and in this moment we're one.

You're reading this and probably thinking I'm half nuts, to which I reply I'm 100 percent nuts, but you'll agree with me on this eventually.

KEGEL EXERCISES

DEFINITION

Kegel exercises are exercises that strengthen a pregnant woman's pelvic floor muscles, which support the uterus, rectum, urethra, and bladder. A gynecologist named Arnold Kegel first recommended that his patients try these moves to retain bladder control during and after pregnancy.

To do Kegel exercises, which can also make sex more enjoyable, women should either sit or lay down and contract the muscles used to stop urination. The pelvic muscle should then be contracted for 3 seconds and relaxed for 3 seconds, about 10–15 times successively.

DADFINITION

Kegel exercises keep the vagina toned during and after the pregnancy on the off chance you'll ever get to see it again.

Oh you'll want to see the vagina, and she'll want to show it to you from time to time, but one of you will be too tired, or too uncomfortable, or hate the way you look or the way you feel or the way the baby sits so quietly when he knows the two of you are trying to have sex in the next room. And when I say "one of you" I mean her. I'll just come right out and say "her."

She'll get over all those hang-ups over time, and you'll be feeling the benefits of those Kegel exercises just in time to try and have another kid.

MEASLES

DEFINITION

Measles (also known as rubeola) is a viral infection that grows in the lungs and throat. It has a variety of symptoms including a runny nose, cough, high fever, and a distinct full-body rash. The rash, which is red and blotchy, begins on the forehead, then spreads down over the rest of the body until it reaches the feet. However, while the rash is very recognizable, one of the first signs of measles is the appearance of Koplik's spots, small red spots that have bluish-white centers that show up in the mouth.

Measles is an airborne virus and is very contagious. Complications can include pneumonia, ear infections, diarrhea, convulsions, and brain damage.

DADFINITION

Measles is one of those scary ailments for which you'll wonder, "How haven't they come up with a cure for this yet?"

Measles can be a devastating disease, especially if it spreads in developing countries where epidemics still occur. Fortunately, the infection is rare in the United States largely due to the effective MMR vaccine, which provides protection against measles, mumps, and rubella. Two shots of this vaccine are currently recommended for children. The first is given at one year, and the second is given when the child is between four and five years of age.

MECONIUM

DEFINITION

Meconium is a thick, green, tar-like substance that is composed of all the materials that the baby ingests while the mother is pregnant, such as amniotic fluid, cells, etc. Meconium is typically released from the baby's intestines during the first few bowel movements after birth.

In some cases, meconium is released prior to birth and inside the womb, which poses a health concern to the baby. In this situation, there is a possibility that the infant will inhale the meconium inside the womb, causing a problem known as meconium aspiration syndrome. If meconium is present during labor, doctors will monitor the infant for signs of fetal distress and may treat the newborn with oxygen and antibiotics, and will suction any meconium out of the lungs.

DADFINITION

Meconium is the blackish-green poop that your baby will excrete in the first few days of life that will freak you the hell out.

As a species, humans tend to do more analyzing of their own feces than we care to admit. The moment our business on the bowl is done, we stand up, glance over our waste, and play pretend doctor using our poop as a guide to self-diagnosis. You mutter phrases like, "That looks normal. I'm probably pretty healthy" or "Holy hell, why am I bleeding out my butt? Oh right, I ate beets last night."

That said, it's no surprise that the first sign of meconium in the baby's diaper will have you on the horn with the pediatrician and searching WebMD for reasons a baby might be crapping road tar. Meconium is just one of the many early-life surprises that will have you wondering if your child is human or a next-generation X-Men mutant.

Eventually, all of the meconium will pass and your kid will be taking healthy human dumps, like a hundred times a day.

And, as you're changing a smelly, dirty diaper for the fiftieth time in what seems like an hour, you'll probably find yourself looking back on meconium with a wistful smile . . . that your partner won't be able to see through your gas mask.

MILIUM CYSTS

DEFINITION

Milium cysts (or milia, when they occur in clusters) are tiny, white bumps that are most commonly found on the cheeks, noses, and eyelids of newborns. Often mistaken for baby acne, the cysts are created when keratin, a common protein, becomes trapped under the skin. Milium cysts in newborns aren't dangerous and will go away in time.

DADFINITION

Milia are small, white bumps that will make any parent who suffered from skin problems revert right back to high school.

Before the birth of a child, many parents mentally tabulate a lengthy list of all their own issues, medical and mental, and hope the child isn't saddled with those same concerns. The list is usually filled with things like acne, attention deficit, legs shorter than the average human, and countless other "problems" parents are fearful will be passed down to their next of kin.

Common medical ailments such as milia can be no cause for concern for a child but might be traumatic for a mother or father with a history of face blemishes. It's important to keep in mind that most ailments in infants will fade over time, and you shouldn't lose your shit over a few small bumps. There are other, more pressing issues to concern yourself with—like keeping that little, bump-covered bundle of joy happy and in one piece.

MONGOLIAN SPOTS

DEFINITION

Mongolian spots are bluish-gray blemishes that resemble bruises, which may randomly appear on a baby's back, buttocks, or legs. Mongolian spots vary in size from no bigger than a penny to over six inches or more in diameter. Mongolian spots are just variations in skin pigment and are not sensitive to the touch. There is no treatment necessary, and the spots will fade over time.

Mongolian spots are much more prevalent in Native American, African American, Asian, and Hispanic children. They are rare in fair-skinned children but do appear from time to time.

DADFINITION

Mongolian spots are odd marks that will put parents into a state of panic and make the parents question either their own handling of their child or accuse others of mishandling or injuring their child.

Random bruises, Mongolian or otherwise, will set off a parent's protective radar. "What are these bruises? Where did they come from? Did someone harm or injure the baby? Please tell me who I'm going to have to murder for the mistreatment of my child!"

Most bruises, bumps, and lumps on a child have a specific medical cause, but because it is automatically assumed in our current "blame someone else for your trouble" culture that harm has been done to a kid, Mongolian spots and other issues are put under the microscopic eyes of a protective parent. Just remember that kids sometimes get bruised when mom or dad aren't watching closely. We're talking about the child who gets tripped by invisible wire and is followed by a fictional sniper. The little dude might just be clumsy and bruises easy, or he may just have Mongolian spots, so breathe easy.

MORO REFLEX

DEFINITION

Commonly known as the "startle reflex" or "startle response," the Moro reflex is the combination of a child's reaction and uncontrolled movement to sudden stimulation or loud noise. The sudden stimulation to the senses causes the child to stiffen her body, thrust her arms and legs outward, then immediately pull the arms and legs back in towards the body.

The pediatrician will check the Moro reflex during the first few wellness visits by placing the child on her back on the examination table. The doctor will lift the head slightly off the table and release, allowing the child to fall back slightly into the doctor's hand. The typical reaction is for the child to have a startled look, extend the arms and legs outward, and possibly cry for a second in momentary fear.

DADFINITION

The Moro reflex is what causes your newborn to flip out when you open the can of soda that you desperately need to keep yourself awake after another sleepless night.

It's basically another reflex check to tell if there is an abnormality in infants without having to run extensive tests. If the Moro reflex isn't present in a newborn, this could mean a broken shoulder bone or damage to the group of nerves that run from the neck and shoulders into the arm. If the Moro reflex is absent from the child, your doctor will most likely call for more testing, usually via an x-ray or MRI, to find the cause of the issue.

NIPPLE CONFUSION

DEFINITION

Nipple confusion is a problem that may occur in babies that are both bottle feeding and breastfeeding where the child forgets how to nurse on the mother's nipple after extended use of bottle nipples or pacifiers.

Because breastfeeding requires the child to suck harder to extract the milk than he would have to if he were drinking from a bottle, switching from the breast to bottle nipples or pacifiers can confuse a newborn who's just learning how to breastfeed. When he goes back onto the breast, the baby becomes easily frustrated.

DADFINITION

Nipple confusion doesn't mean your kid forgets what the breasts do, or which breasts belong to him, but it's more about not being able to adjust back to the breasts after being given bottles and vice versa. Here's where there will be no confusion at all—those human nipples no longer belong to dad.

Nipple confusion can be just as frustrating to mom as it is to the child. To avoid the situation, it's best to keep the child exclusively on the breast until breastfeeding becomes commonplace and routine.

Remember this handy rhyme—bottle before boob, he'll look like a noob; boob before bottle, he'll go full throttle. I have no idea if that will help, but it will at least make it look like you're trying.

NURSING PILLOW

DEFINITION

A nursing pillow, also referred to as a breastfeeding pillow, is a C-shaped pillow that provides a mother with support for both her back and arm while she's breastfeeding. These pillows, which were first used to help babies sit up unassisted, also help a breastfeeding mother settle her baby into an efficient nursing position.

If a baby is held in the incorrect position while feeding, she could have problems swallowing or develop gastric reflux. Nursing pillows help put the baby in the best position to prevent these issues.

DADFINITION

The nursing pillow helps mothers hold babies when breastfeeding and help fathers hold the baby when they're trying to do other things while caring for said baby.

As a father, you'll find other uses for the nursing pillow as it will allow a sleeping child to stay on your lap while you're playing video games, flipping channels and watching TV, or when you're giving a bottle and just too damn tired to hold the kid.

The C shape of the nursing pillow, sold under the names Boppy and My Brest Friend (yes, seriously), is also perfect for resting the child inside without the possible danger of the kid rolling away or grabbing the controller during an incredibly intense moment in Halo 5.

After the baby outgrows the nursing pillow, fathers are encouraged to hang onto them to use as head pillows for sleeping upright on the couch or to place just above their massive guts as a place to rest drinks and snacks.

OBJECT PERMANENCE

DEFINITION

Object permanence is the understanding that an object can disappear from sight but still exists.

Jean Piaget, a Swiss psychologist, first studied the concept of object permanence in children and considered it "an infant's most important accomplishment." In Piaget's studies, there are six stages of object permanence that range from one month to two years of age.

- Reflex schema stage (0–1 months): Babies learn how the body moves and works and aren't yet aware of objects to know they exist or have disappeared from sight.
- Primary circular reactions (1–4 months): Babies begin to notice objects and follow their movements. They look to the spot where an object was, but only for a moment, before searching and finding it again.
- Secondary circular reactions (4–8 months): If an object is partially hidden, a child will reach for that object, indicating the child knows it still exists even if he can't visually see the object.
- Coordination of secondary circular reactions (8–12 months): The child recognizes an object that has just been hidden and makes an attempt to retrieve the object.
- Tertiary circular reactions (12–18 months): The child is able to retrieve an object when it's hidden out of view, but must see the object when it is hidden in order to retrieve the object.
- Invention of new means through mental coordination (18–24 months): The child is now able to reason out where an object may be and is able to retrieve an object when it is hidden inside a container

DADFINITION

Object permanence: the scientific concept that shows you that the hidden toy trick is actually a learning process. But this doesn't make peekaboo any less entertaining—especially when you're working on a few nights of little to no sleep.

In recent years, studies have emerged refuting some of Piaget's findings and proving that infants much younger than three months can recognize the fact that an object still exists even if it's taken out of sight. Even so, the most important takeaway from Piaget's research and the idea and the concept of object permanence is that your child is learning even when you're doing something as simple as hiding his favorite toy under a blanket or putting it behind your back.

PACIFIER

DEFINITION

Known by many different names—binkies, binks, dummies, and soothers—the pacifier is large enough that a small child won't choke on or swallow it, and it often prevents children from putting other objects in their mouth to suck on.

There are several advantages and disadvantages to pacifier use with newborns. Babies who use pacifiers at bedtime and naptime have a reduced risk of sudden infant death syndrome, or SIDS, and pacifiers also keep children from sucking their thumb to soothe themselves, a habit that is much harder to break. The disadvantages are that the child might have trouble sleeping without one, and some studies have shown an increased possibility of ear infections in kids who use pacifiers.

DADFINITION

A pacifier is mom and dad's best friend . . . until it becomes their biggest nightmare.

Pacifiers often solve all problems and heal all wounds: tiredness, crankiness, anger, sadness, pain, and even boredom. The baby wakes up crying in the middle of the night, pop a bink in her mouth, and, *boom*, she's out cold until morning.

FICTIONAL BUT FUNNY

OVER-THE-TOP TOT (OTTT)

Everyone knows an OTTT. They're always wearing the latest "it" baby gear, complete with accessories, such as blinged-up binkies and bespoke baby booties. They also travel in only the finest transportation.

Warning—the day the binkie gets taken away forever will be a sad day. Buckets and buckets of tears shall be shed. Seriously, you're going to cry for hours. *"But how will the kid sleep?!? The kid needs to sleep so I can sleep!!!!"*

The baby will get over the pacifier long before you get over not being able to give the kid a pacifier. Just don't crack under pressure, because the longer you wait, the harder it gets. Be strong. Be tough. Stop crying. The kid is watching.

PALMAR GRASP REFLEX

DEFINITION

The palmar grasp reflex is when an infant automatically closes her entire hand around an object placed in her palm. This reflex shows itself at birth and remains until the baby is five or six months old.

Even though the palmar grasp is reflexive and strong, it's not very reliable. The child will be mainly unaware that an item has been grabbed and her hand will release the item without warning.

DADFINITION

The palmar grasp reflex is the first thing you'll use to teach your kid cool tricks. "Watch what happens when I stroke his palm! Watch what happens when I show him my keys! Watch what happens when I let him use the vacuum cleaner!"

The palmar grasp is the first glimpse into just how strong an infant can be, especially when it comes to grip. You'll realize this when it takes you a good five minutes to get the remote control out of your daughter's hand. She's got a vise-like grip . . . and you really need to set the DVR! It'll only be a matter of time before she's wrestling you to the ground and bullying you for all those years you used her reflexes as a party trick.

PARENTAL LEAVE

DEFINITION

Parental leave or family leave is an employee benefit that provides time off work to care for a child or make arrangements for the child's welfare. The terms "parental leave" and "family leave" include paid maternity, paternity, and adoption leave. Often, the minimum benefits are stipulated by law.

Paid parental leave has been available as a legal right and/or governmental program for many years, in one form or another, in most countries. However, in a handful of countries, like Papua New Guinea, Suriname, Liberia, and the good old United States of America, parental leave provides only unpaid time off work. The United States is the only developed nation not to provide paid parental leave.

DADFINITION

Parental leave is one of those rare instances when Americans feel way, way behind the rest of the world.

If you're trying to make ends meet in the United States, you should know that this won't be the first time as a parent you'll feel as though the deck is stacked against you. There will be many rules and laws that feel like they exclude parents and young children. If you're not living in the United States and enjoyed or are enjoying the benefit of an income while you're home with your baby, at some point, you'll still feel as though the odds are stacked against you.

In the end, we're all on the same page.

FICTIONAL BUT FUNNY

MOMPRENEUR

A mom who spends half her time caring for kids and the rest of the time trying to run a business from her home.

PEDIATRICIAN

DEFINITION

A pediatrician is a doctor who specializes in the care of children under the age of twenty-one. The pediatrician is the first person to call whenever your child is sick or exhibiting a sign of prolonged sickness or health issues.

The pediatrician will see your child once every few months from birth until the age of three for "wellness" visits. From the age of three on, your pediatrician will see your child every year for annual checkups.

DADFINITION

The pediatrician is the doctor who'll see your child when he's sick or when he's well and is the person who won't judge you (to your face) if you bring your child to the office in a panic because he's running a low-grade fever. If your kid goes to daycare at a young age, you'll see the pediatrician way too often because daycares are tiny buildings full of disease.

You'll have a love-hate relationship with your pediatrician until your kid is old enough to see an adult doctor or until you find a new pediatrician. Why? Well, you'll likely find yourself searching for answers as to why your kid is sick all the time, developing slower than other kids his age, or whatever other issues (real or imagined) you think the kid has. When the pediatrician isn't able to instantly fix the problem, chances are you'll get pretty angry. The problem is people think pediatricians are the fixers, but they're not. They're just the people who can diagnose and come up with a treatment plan. The sooner you realize that, the happier—and less rage filled—you'll be.

REFLUX

DEFINITION

Reflux, technically called gastroesophageal reflux, occurs in babies when swallowed milk comes back up into either the esophagus or the mouth. Reflux can occur with both formula-fed and breastfed babies.

Roughly half of all newborns have reflux once or more a day during their first three months, but reflux is a temporary problem that usually gets better on its own. However, a small percentage of babies will suffer from severe or persistent reflux, known as gastroesophageal reflux disease, and will require medical attention.

DADFINITION

Reflux is a pretty intense situation that typically leaves you covered in regurgitated milk or formula, wondering if your kid is actually getting anything to eat.

The good thing is that reflux in kids isn't much different than the reflux suffered by countless adults except in babies it's slightly more frustrating because the kid can't just pop a Nexium.

If your baby is on formula, try switching around to different brands, as it might be as simple as one type of formula giving the kid more heartburn than another. If the child is on strictly breast milk, try and switch to a new partner. It won't happen, but just try, for your kid's sake.

You can also try holding the baby in different positions during feeding, to make the flow of milk through the esophagus and down to the stomach much easier. The perfect position for my baby was in the arms of his mother who was better at it than I was.

ROOTING

DEFINITION

Rooting is a newborn feeding reflex that causes the child to turn her head toward a finger or nipple (bottle or otherwise) that brushes against her lips or the side of her face.

Babies aren't born with the ability to know how to eat, but they are born with the rooting reflex as a means of letting their parents know when they might be hungry.

The rooting reflex can help a breastfed baby latch on to the breast and a formula-fed baby grab the bottle nipple. A simple stroke of the cheek can cause the child to begin to root, making feeding (especially breast-feeding) slightly easier.

DADFINITION

Rooting is usually one of the early signs that your child is hungry. Besides sucking on her fingers or fists, rooting is one of the easiest signs that it's time for the baby to eat.

Crying is usually the final signal from the child, saying, "Hey, how about a little grub?" If you're holding the baby and the other signs start to creep in, it's probably time to hand her over to momma or reach for the bottle.

Here's a word of warning for dads: The baby doesn't care where the food is coming from and doesn't know the difference between your nipple and your partner's (even though your areola is considerably hairier), so if your partner is breastfeeding, be careful the kid doesn't latch on either with mouth or hands to your chest. It smarts more than you imagine.

ROSEOLA

DEFINITION

Roseola is a fairly mild illness caused by a type of the herpes virus. It is very common and typically occurs in children between the ages of six months and three years old. Roseola is contagious and is spread through the fluids of the infected person while he is asymptomatic.

Roseola sometimes begins with what looks like an upper respiratory illness, but some children don't present any symptoms until they develop the sudden, relatively high fever—often over 103°F—associated with the virus. The fever lasts three to five days and is followed by roseola's telltale rash, which appears right as the fever breaks and lasts up to a few days. The rash is made up of flat pink spots or raised pink bumps. These spots or bumps may be a lighter color at their edges and will turn white if you press on them. While intense looking, the rash won't be uncomfortable and it won't itch.

DADFINITION

Unlike other rashes, roseola is a virus accompanied by a high fever, and fevers always freak parents out.

It's usually because baby fevers tend to go so high. A 101°F fever on a baby is cause for some concern, but babies tend to run a little hotter than adults. A 101°F fever on an adult and you're calling out of work for the next month and Googling potential spots you might have picked up Ebola. And if this is the case, the 103°F fever associated with roseola is really going to make you go nuts.

Keep your cool, though. Once the fever dies down and you see the rash moving in, the roseola is on its way out. Just monitor your child and everything will be okay.

SEPARATION ANXIETY

DEFINITION

Separation anxiety is a normal, developmentally appropriate stage of life where the child becomes very upset and worried when she is away from her parents or another caregiver like a grandparent, or is away from home. The anxiety typically begins at around nine months of age but can start as early as six months or as late as one year. Some kids pass through this stage quickly, but for others, it could last for almost six months to a year.

DADFINITION

Separation anxiety is the fear of being out in the world alone even when there's nothing to fear at all.

The effects of this developmental stage on you are twofold: First, it will cause you to love your kids even more because you know they love you so much that they're devastated when you have to leave for work or even to use the restroom. Secondly, you'll want to pull your hair out because every time you head out the door you're faced with ear-piercing screams, devastated faces, and what seems like absolutely irrational behavior.

Perhaps the best approach to the separation anxiety issue is to reassure your child that you're not leaving forever. Sometimes that's all a kid needs to hear.

SOCIAL WORKER

DEFINITION

Social workers are trained professionals who help families coordinate social services through various private and government agencies to help families access programs such as WIC, early intervention programs, and more. They also help families understand and use their insurance coverage. In addition, many social workers also act as counselors for parents who have a child in the NICU (neonatal intensive care unit) at the hospital.

DADFINITION

Social workers are people who care more about other people than you do. They are the people who are willing to help out families and children who are having a hard time helping themselves.

Imagine everything you deal with in life—work, family, personal goals, financial worries—and now imagine worrying about that for count-less other people, most of them strangers who probably don't thank you enough for all that you do. That's the life of a social worker. Top it all off with all of the heartbreaking things they see on any given day.

Social workers are the unsung heroes in the world, not just because of their work with kids and families in need, but because of the host of other people they help day in and day out.

SOUND MACHINE

DEFINITION

A sound machine is a device that produces a variety of calming sounds. Its most central function is usually its ability to produce white noise, which masks other sounds and can be helpful in aiding sleep. Most sound machines also have the ability to produce a few other noises, especially natural sounds like rainfall, ocean waves, and wind.

Parents often place sound machines next to a child's bed while he sleeps. The machines are generally made to be small and unobtrusive. They usually have some kind of volume control and a method for selecting different sounds. The pricier models will normally have more sound options, while the less expensive models may only offer white noise or possibly one or two additional settings.

DADFINITION

A sound machine is a device used to keep the sounds outside a kid's room from creeping their way inside.

Sound machines are used to soothe a child to sleep much the same way they work on adults. White noise machine use with newborns took a dip a few years back when a study was released stating that sound machine usage might cause hearing issues for kids later in life. Might. Might cause hearing issues. The researchers failed to make it clear that the study wasn't actually conducted on children.

Sound machines (the jungle setting) are used in both my kids' rooms because of the age of our house. Every door closing, entrance and exit into a room, or mouse fart echoes throughout the house waking both kids. If this sounds like your home, try using a sound machine. It will keep your kids asleep, and if you place it far enough away from their beds and at a low enough volume, you won't have to worry about any hearing issues when they get older. Besides, by the time they're teens, headphones will go so deep into the ear and play at such an obscene level that it might be better if their hearing goes now.

STORK BITES

DEFINITION

The nevus simplex, commonly called the stork bite, is a reddish birthmark that appears on about one-third of all newborns. Stork bites are caused by a stretching or dilation of certain blood vessels that change color depending on the child's mood or on various environmental changes. The stork bite may become darker or redder when the child cries or the temperature changes.

A baby can be born with a stork bite, but often they appear in the first months of life. They're commonly found on the forehead, eyelids, nose, upper lip, or back of the neck.

A doctor can diagnose a stork bite simply by looking at it, and additional tests or treatment aren't typically needed. If a stork bite lasts longer than three years, it can be removed through laser treatment.

DADFINITION

Stork bites are pink, flat marks found on your child that work as good external indicators of how uncomfortable or pissed off your child is at any moment.

While the stork bite may bother you when your child is initially born, soon you'll be able to use it as an early warning system. If you're in a public place and you notice your baby's stork bite turning red, you know that a screaming fit is going to ensue and have time to make it out of the store before said fit occurs. Or say you dress your toddler in something that you think is appropriate for the outside temperature, but when his stork bite starts to flash red, you realize that you need to pull that hoodie off of him ASAP. Stork bites disappear over time, so use them to your best advantage while you still can.

I was born with a stork bite that still appears right in the middle of my head, in the spot between the eyes and above the bridge of the nose. As a kid, the spot would get dark and red when I was angry, about to tantrum, or was seconds away from losing my mind and falling into a fit of crying. My strawberry mark now appears before my kids do any or all of those things in a public place.

SWADDLING

DEFINITION

Swaddling is the act of wrapping a baby in a blanket or swaddling sack in order to keep her calm, secure, and warm and to help her sleep.

Swaddling keeps the baby's arms compressed to the body in a way that mimics the snugness of the womb. This position helps the baby feel safe and may also keep her from being disturbed or awakened by her startle reflex, the combination of a child's reaction and uncontrolled movement to sudden stimulation or loud noise.

It's very important that you learn how to swaddle correctly and leave the legs and hips loose. Incorrect positioning in the swaddle can cause loose joints and hip dysplasia.

DADFINITION

Swaddling is the technique of tightly wrapping a blanket around a child so that not even baby Houdini himself can escape.

Once parents master the swaddle, a decent night's sleep for both baby and mom and dad can be had. If swaddling with a blanket is impossible, there are swaddling jackets available that make the act easy for even a swaddling novice. It's like a Velcro straightjacket for babies that keeps them warm and cozy and, more importantly, quiet so you can get some much-needed sleep yourself.

TEETHING

DEFINITION

Teething is the process by which an infant's teeth break through the gums. Also referred to as the "cutting" of the teeth (or odontiasis if you want to use the medical term), teething usually begins between four and six months of age and should be over by the time the child turns three years old.

Besides the now-showing teeth, there are several signs or symptoms associated with teething, including irritability, tender and swollen gums, and the constant need for the child to put toys, objects, or fingers into his mouth in an attempt to reduce discomfort.

Over-the-counter pain relievers such as infant acetaminophen or infant ibuprofen generally provide a level of relief for most of the teething symptoms, but the pain can also be relieved by letting the child chew on a cold facecloth or hard teething biscuit.

DADFINITION

Teething is when your child is in pain and can't communicate to make it better, and you're in pain because the teething keeps him (and you!) up at night, prevents him from napping, or just puts him in a mood for most of the day. Medicines (for the baby, not the parents) will dull the pain, but the discomfort will be back once the medicines wear off.

Unfortunately, teething is just one of the many "growing pains" that your child will experience that you have little control over and are almost powerless to stop from becoming an uncomfortable situation for all.

It's likely that you'll be yanking out your teeth to cope with the pain of his growing in. If only you could rub whiskey on it like your grandfather did to your old man. Maybe instead you can drink the whiskey. At least you'll sleep through the night.

TUMMY TIME

DEFINITION

Tummy time is the act of placing a newborn on her stomach in order to help her build strong head, neck, and shoulder muscles and advanced motor skills.

Tummy time can begin about a month after birth and gives the child a different view of the world than the customary view on her back.

There really is no set amount of time, but doctors suggest no longer than ten minutes a couple of times a day. Tummy time should always be supervised, and when the child begins to fuss or express frustration, it's time to pick her up or roll her over on her back.

DADFINITION

Tummy time is a good change of scenery for the child and for dads. Watching a child wiggle around on her back is kind of like watching PBS—it's important but boring as hell after a while.

Tummy time is an early sign that a child is beginning to develop into something besides a pooping paperweight. The child will lift her head up, attempt to push her body off the ground, and do just about anything to prevent the eventual face full of carpet coming her way. Tummy time is also a good bonding experience once the child begins to push herself up, keep her head upright, and look into her father's eyes with the look of "Why the hell are you torturing me with these primitive calisthenics? I want to lie down all day like you do. You jerk."

TWINS

DEFINITION

Twins are two babies who are born from the same mother at (relatively) the same time. There are two different types of twins that a mother can have:

- Fraternal twins: Fraternal twins, also called dizygotic twins, come about when two different eggs are fertilized by two different sperm. These twins may or may not be of the same sex, and are not any more similar in appearance than they would be to other siblings, even though they share the uterus during development.
- Identical twins: Identical twins, also called monozygotic twins, come about when one fertilized egg splits into two separate embryos. These twins are always the same sex and also share the same genetic makeup, including blood type. According to the American Society of Reproductive Medicine, identical twins occur in 1 of every 250 births and make up 33 percent of all twin births. The incidence of identical twin pregnancies is similar for all races and age groups.

Twins, no matter the type, have a higher risk of complications and a higher chance of being born prematurely due to the stress multiple babies put on the mother's body.

DADFINITION

Twins are something that everyone wants to have until the realization sets in that two newborn babies at one time are about to happen.

Case in point, I once said very foolishly in the early stages of my wife's pregnancy that I hoped she was having twins to "get the two kids over with in one shot."

What. A. Moron.

Parents of twins, triplets, and anything higher than three kids at once are amazing people who have been blessed not just with multiple children but a massive chunk of patience. I lost my cool over one newborn, and I can't imagine adding another newborn or *multiple newborns* into the mix. I would have cried all night long with the kids the first night that no one slept.

FICTIONAL BUT FUNNY

IRISH TWINS

Children born in succession within one year, because mom and dad couldn't wait to have another child.

WEANING

DEFINITION

Weaning is the process of gradually replacing a baby's liquid diet (breast milk or formula) with solid foods. The term "weaning" is used more commonly to refer to the transition from breast milk to solids, but it is also used when the baby transitions off the bottle.

The two common types of weaning are baby-led weaning, which is when the child shows signs that it's time to stop nursing and bottle feeding, and mother-led weaning, which is when mom decides it's time to stop these practices.

DADFINITION

Weaning means a child needs to find other ways to eat and catch some shuteye, which is too bad because babies are creatures of habit.

When you wean your baby, you slowly take away his method of choice to calm down or fall asleep. This is too bad, but mom can't be a human milk machine forever and your kid can't bring a bottle to first grade, so eventually he needs to say goodbye to both breast and bottle.

Regular food or formula in a sippy cup is the easiest way to feed a weaning kid, but what about the comfort of sucking down a liquid meal at bedtime? The kid needs a distraction, something to take his mind off it. Try all the same things that worked for you—baseball or just sobbing gently under the covers. Or maybe just read the kid a book or cuddle.

PART 3

THE REST OF YOUR LIFE

You're going to wake up one day and realize you're not just caring for a child anymore, but are raising a person who will become a functioning member of society. How functional depends on how good of a job you've done so far. No pressure.

As your child grows, the two of you will discover amazing new things. You'll discover that you've lost a sizable chunk of time raising a kid and will begin to explore your own personal interests. Your child will do the same. Those interests and hobbies sometimes even match up. What luck!

In this section of the book, you'll learn all about a variety of popular parenting strategies, and you'll find the info you need on parental rights, product recalls, and countless other buzzwords that you'll encounter on the very long road of parenting left ahead.

ANTIBIOTICS

DEFINITION

"Antibiotic" is the term for the more than 100 medications that are prescribed to treat bacterial infections. Antibiotics can kill bacteria and/or keep it from growing in the body. Once the harmful bacteria is successfully eliminated, the infection clears up, and the child returns to health.

Some common childhood illnesses helped by antibiotics include:

- Strep throat
- Pneumonia

- Severe acne
- Sinus infections

Antibiotics cannot help treat the majority of colds, flus, or other childhood illnesses.

DADFINITION

Antibiotics are medications that parents give to their children when they're really sick, and then stop giving when they feel better . . . whether the prescription has been finished or not.

It's human nature to not worry about something that's not right in front of your face, but it is important with all antibiotics to finish the entire prescription and not just when the issue seems to subside or starts to get better. Take it from a dad who's been tricked many times by the "He seems fine" early positive reactions to an antibiotic.

You stop giving the kid the meds, it seems as though the issue goes away, and, *boom*, he's back on the DL because dad thinks he's a doctor instead of just reading the directions on the damn bottle. Finish the meds even if the kid puts up a fight. You can take him. Did you hear that cough? It will be a piece of cake.

ATTACHMENT PARENTING

DEFINITION

"Attachment parenting" refers to a style of responsive parenting that intends to create a secure attachment between a child and parent that leads to a more independent child. This parenting style is based on the developmental psychology principles of attachment theory.

There are eight key principles to attachment parenting. Attachment Parenting International, an association that teaches attachment parenting worldwide, identifies these principles as follows:

- To prepare for pregnancy, birth, and parenting with positivity and love
- To breastfeed the child to inspire love, respect, and connection
- To respond to the child's emotions with sensitivity and love
- To always use a nurturing touch and encourage skin-to-skin contact and babywearing
- To engage in nighttime parenting by cosleeping with the child
- To provide constant and loving care no matter where or what the parent is doing in life
- To practice positive discipline and ensure that disagreements or tantrums are used as learning opportunities to facilitate emotional growth
- To maintain balance in their personal and family life

Few parents incorporate all eight of these principles. Most tend to take a trial-and-error approach to each and use the ones that work best for their family and lifestyle.

DADFINITION

Attachment parenting is an intense parenting style that can cause even the most patient parents to throw up their hands. It calls for mom and dad to take on a ton of responsibility for the kids without allowing for a support network of friends, family, or just a babysitter to come over so mom and dad can go live a little.

Another difficulty that may arise in attachment parenting is that, while it could be beneficial for the child because of the bond to the parent that it creates, it might actually cause the child to take a little bit longer to venture out on his own. It might take him, well, forever. Attachment parenting might also crush a parent's will to be an individual with his own personal interests because he's too busy being everything to his child.

That said, if you can handle it, consider giving attachment parenting a try. If you can't, it's fine to take parts of this parenting style and mix and match them into what works for you as you see fit. No parenting style is perfect.

FICTIONAL BUT FUNNY

OFF(SPRING) BREAK

A break you take from your kids where you *talk* about getting drunk and naked with your partner but really just go to Ikea for four blissful hours and to a restaurant without a children's menu. It's almost as good as sex.

AU PAIR

DEFINITION

An au pair is a person who works as an assistant inside the home to provide live-in childcare in return for a place to stay free of charge and a small salary. The term, meaning "equal to" or "at par," indicates that the person is equal to others in the family, almost like an adopted member.

Originating in Europe, the term "au pair" typically describes a student who works for a family part time while studying and going to school the rest of the time. In the United States, au pairs generally work as full-time caretakers.

Au pairs are usually expected to do a variety of duties related to the care of the children. Many au pairs are expected to care for the kids, cook for them, do their laundry, clean up after them, and sometimes even put them to bed. An au pair's duties end with the child, and an au pair is never expected to do any of those duties for members of the family besides the children.

DADFINITION

Au pair is a French way of saying "your kid's butler."

Au pairs are more common in affluent areas of the country, but more families are incorporating them into daily childcare because their rates are sometimes cheaper than afterschool care or babysitters. An au pair is often considered to be a healthier daycare option for a child

> ### FICTIONAL BUT FUNNY
>
> #### AU PAIRANOIA
>
> The nagging feeling that the au pair is much better at raising your kids than you are.

because an au pair is a "member of the family" who takes care of the kid's needs.

Au pairs are usually obtained through a third-party company that specializes in the screening and qualifying of the au pair and will match the best candidate with the needs of your family to alleviate the pressure of finding an au pair on your own.

Another advantage to employing an au pair is the exposure of your child to a person with a much different culture and background since most au pairs hail from different countries.

AUTHORITARIAN PARENTING

DEFINITION

Authoritarian parenting is a disciplinary parenting style in which a mother and father make their children follow their explicit instructions and expect the children to have the utmost respect for their work and effort.

Also known as a "Tiger Mom" (taken from the controversial but popular book), an authoritarian parent is extremely strict and controlling and often uses punishment as the main form of discipline (no cooling-off periods here). Authoritarian parents have high standards for their children and expect them to be very high achieving. They also have very strict rules regarding what is and isn't acceptable. These parents are stereotypically cold toward their children and rarely give the kids choices or options in life.

Obedience is stressed and discussion is discouraged. There isn't any wiggle room in the eyes of an authoritarian parent.

DADFINITION

Authoritarian parenting is a softer way to say "dictatorship."

Authoritarian parents are often the offspring of other authoritarian parents and really don't know any other way of parenting. The children who rebel often rebel with dire consequences, but that doesn't stop this parenting philosophy from surviving generation after generation. It's a personal choice of parenting style, and those parents who practice it have to live with the outcome and possible consequences.

Knock authoritarian parenting if you like, but there's no denying that kids from an authoritarian household are more successful in school, and then, in life. I'm sure they're very happy about all of their success. I'd ask a kid, but he's too scared to talk to me, or move, or blink.

AUTHORITATIVE PARENTING

DEFINITION

Authoritative parenting is a democratic, kidcentric way to raise a child where parents expect their children to achieve but are willing to give the emotional support the child needs on the path to success.

Authoritative parents take a moderate approach to raising children and set high standards for kids while also respecting their individuality enough to allow them to question and rationalize rules, rewards, and punishments.

Authoritative parents are flexible, listen to their child in situations of conflict, and allow a child to explain her side of the situation. These parents will then adjust their response to the situation accordingly.

DADFINITION

Authoritative parenting is a middle-of-the-road parenting style that every mother and father hopes to adopt.

Parents want to believe they approach parenting with a democratic philosophy, but try as they may, most parents tend to lean either towards authoritarian or permissive parenting. Why? Well, it's incredibly difficult to approach every situation with a child with a democratic mindset. First off, kids lie like hell. Adults lie! Why wouldn't a child? Even if you want to treat a kid like an adult, she's going to do anything to cover her butt. Authoritative parenting gives a kid the benefit of the doubt until the kid screws up for the hundredth time.

BABY GATE

DEFINITION

A baby gate is a protective barrier that has been designed to keep kids out of unsafe areas.

Baby gates, which are commonly made out of plastic, metal, and/or wood, are designed to be used either indoors or outdoors. There are a variety of gates available, but most are either hardware or pressure mounted. Most baby gates are pressure mounted and typically held in place by walls on either side. Some gates are hardware mounted and screw into the wall studs with a fully swinging door to allow adult access. Most gates can be expanded to fit a variety of doorways.

DADFINITION

Baby gates are designed to protect a child from roaming too far away from a parent, but sometimes a baby gate also works to shield a parent from a clingy child.

Baby gates are perfect to give you some time away from a crawling, cruising, or attached-at-the-hip kid when you just need to get away for five minutes. Try not to look down as the child grabs onto the gate like an inmate at Alcatraz and begs you to free him from his temporary holding cell.

In addition to giving you some space and keeping your kid out of dangerous situations, baby gates can also keep your kid contained in certain rooms like the bedroom or a bathroom when you have stuff to do in there and don't want your kid to roam too far away. Be careful, though; baby-gating a child into a bathroom could be considered torture depending on the available ventilation—and what you had for dinner.

BABY SIGN LANGUAGE

DEFINITION

Baby sign language is a simplified version of sign language that parents use to communicate with infants and toddlers. In baby sign language, a child is only taught a limited number of manual signs that can stand alone to communicate her needs.

Advocates of baby sign language believe that the lag time between the desire to communicate and the time a baby develops the verbal skills to do this often causes frustration and anger. Sign language eliminates this issue because it allows a nonverbal child to communicate simple and most common requests, such as *more, eat, sleep*, and *hug*.

DADFINITION

Baby sign language is a way to communicate with your baby that decreases the instances when exasperation leaves you with no other choice but to scream at the top of your lungs, *"Just tell me what the hell you want!"*

I'm an advocate of using baby sign language to communicate with your child, and of using a full arsenal of signs to communicate with your partner when your baby gets too old to talk about certain topics in front of him.

Baby sign language is also a missed opportunity for college students. If only you'd thought of learning sign language on those mornings you were too hung over to leave your dorm room. You could have signed "food, drink, stuffed bear" to your roommate instead of just pointing, getting angry when he didn't understand, and throwing a bag full of textbooks at his face.

BATHROOM TALK

DEFINITION

Also referred to as potty mouth, bathroom talk occurs when a child incorporates bathroom and bodily functions into everyday conversation.

The reason for the upswing in the use of words like "poop," "butt," and "fart" is twofold. First, these words tend to elicit a response (usually a laugh) from adults, and laughter is a form of positive reinforcement for kids. Children typically don't care why an adult (or sometimes a friend or classmate) is laughing, just that he is laughing, and the laughter causes a positive reinforcement.

The second reason for the sudden dropping of dirty words into simple requests for ice cream ("I'll take the butt flavor") or answers about the lessons in school ("Today in school we learned about flowers and some of them smelled like poop") is because the words feel off-limits since they're only used by adults when discussing actual toilet training.

DADFINITION

Bathroom talk is when your kid starts hilariously sprinkling words like "fart," "poop," and "penis" into casual conversation. The typical male reaction is to laugh hysterically, because who doesn't love a good fart gag, but the secondary reaction depends on just how serious you take the issue.

Every kid uses bathroom language and flashes moments of potty mouth. If you see it as a big deal, sit your child down and explain why certain words shouldn't be said in public or in regular conversation. If you don't see it as a big deal, chuckle and move the conversation on to a different topic. The bigger your reaction, the more times you're going to hear the potty talk, because your child is only interested in getting the reaction.

If you consider potty talk to be a serious issue, feel free to consult a professional about how to eliminate the words from your child's vocabulary. But honestly, you're just making this a bigger deal than it is, so just stop being such a turd about it.

BOOSTER SEAT

DEFINITION

A booster seat is an object that elevates a child to an appropriate height. There are a couple of different ways a booster seat is used:

- In the car: When used in the car, a booster seat is an item that makes sure your child is seated in such a way that the seat belt is appropriately fastened over and around the child. Unlike car seats, which have a five-point harness system, booster seats rely on the vehicle's seat belt system to restrain the child in the car. Booster seats should only be used in the backseat for safety.
- At the table: The term "booster seat" may also refer to the elevated seats placed on chairs around dining room tables and in restaurants. These allow the child to sit and eat at the table instead of in a highchair.

DADFINITION

Booster seats are the phone books of today.

In the past, maybe a kid sat on the Yellow Pages in order to reach the table or just winged it in the car, but today's booster seats are a good way to elevate your child physically and to also elevate her feelings of being a "big kid."

Booster seats in the car allow the child to move a little more freely, take in the scenes speeding past the window, and engage with other people in the car. Booster seats at dining tables allow the child to feed herself and feel like a part of the family, not a diner sitting at a different table a few feet away.

Booster seats are just another sign that your kid is growing up. They're also a great excuse to take the highchair out to the backyard and rip it into a hundred different pieces. Highchairs are the worst. You'll see.

BRIBERY

DEFINITION

Bribery is the (typically dishonest) act of giving someone a gift as a way to change his or her behavior.

Bribery is a popular parenting technique that is used to either get a child to start doing something or to get a child to stop doing something. Although bribing a child can get her to do or not do what you want to achieve a desired result, those results are typically short-lived. In fact, bribery can also cause a cycle of bad behavior where the child acts out in anticipation of receiving another bribe.

DADFINITION

Bribery is a way to get your kids to stop acting up or acting out even when they might be doing just that—acting.

Many parents are fans of bribery at first because it does just what it's intended to do—stop a kid from doing whatever wrong thing she's doing. That's great until you notice that your kid just does the same wrong things over and over again. If your kid is anything like my kid, she's much too bright to do the same thing over and over unless she knows the eventual result. She gets a toy just for acting like a brat. It's a no-lose situation . . . for her. For you, it's just a situation where you have to deal with the monster you've created.

It's hard to break the cycle of bribery, but it will end up costing you and your kid more than entire paychecks at a toy store if you don't steel yourself against your child's screams and stop the bribes.

COMPETENCE

DEFINITION

Competence is what parents give to children when they raise them to have the resilience, adaptability, and self-assurance to jump into activities and projects, do what needs to be done to complete a task, and stay positive when things don't go according to plan.

Competent children are kids without emotional baggage who are able to confidently move through the stages of their lives in developmentally appropriate ways, learn from those stages, and use those experiences to grow. These confident, resourceful kids believe that they can achieve anything they put their minds to and are able to roll with the punches when things get tough.

DADFINITION

Competence teaches a child to tackle a task from start to finish—even if dad is clueless how to do this himself.

The best way to teach children competence, or any life skill for that matter, is to set a good example. You want your kids to be resilient, adaptable, and able to tackle life's biggest obstacles while you sit back and let those obstacles kick you in the face on a daily basis. Sure, adult life is different than the life of a kid because adulthood brings with it many more ramifications and much bigger hurdles. But if you can't turn back around and kick life in the teeth, why do you expect your kid to be able to?

Either take skills like competence to heart and learn them yourself, or take inspiration from your child who has the world by the nuts while you're busy protecting yours.

CONCERTED CULTIVATION

DEFINITION

Concerted cultivation is a parenting style in which parents attempt to raise cultured, disciplined children who are capable of navigating the adult world at a young age.

These children, who are often enrolled in a large number of after-school programs designed to nurture their innate talents, learn how to interact with and question authority figures, which allows them to feel comfortable moving in the adult world. This interaction helps these children cultivate vital reasoning and critical-thinking skills.

The philosophy behind concerted cultivation is that this parenting strategy prepares children for the future by telling them that they have to work hard now and then enjoy the fruits of their labor later on. The parents who practice concerted cultivation believe that the work put into activities like sports, musical instruments, and study as a child pays off in a financially lucrative career.

DADFINITION

Concerted cultivation believes in work hard now, play later, which sounds great, but cultivated kids never really learn how to play later. Concerted cultivation is really "work hard now, work harder later, buy things that are fun, but barely ever touch them since you're still working hard to afford more things to play with."

It's fine for kids to work hard at a skill, but it's important to let a kid have fun at the same time. The danger of pushing too many activities on a kid is that the things that were once fun—gymnastics, guitar, and dancing—soon become a job.

Concerted cultivation not only consumes the child's free time but also your spare time as well, which is now spent driving kids to practices, recitals, and programs to fill the time. You and your partner need organized free time as much as kids, so try to coordinate a time where your entire family is expected to do absolutely nothing.

CONSISTENCY

DEFINITION

Consistency, as a parent, means ensuring that key parts of your child's life remain the same from one day to the next. Consistency gives children a sense of security because they know what to expect. They also learn that they can rely on their parents to meet their daily needs, over and over again, which allows them to trust and bond with their parents and eliminates any anxiety about what will happen.

Consistency, which involves daily routines, rules, and consequences in regards to rising from and going to bed, mealtimes, and appropriate behavior, teaches children how to behave appropriately and follow the rules, which will, ultimately, translate over to a peaceful, calm routine in the home.

DADFINITION

Consistency is something that you know you should do but aren't consistent enough to follow through on. You see, the key to consistency is consistency. Sound confusing? Then allow this modern-day Confucius to explain: It's incredibly difficult to be consistent because sometimes life gets in the way or a parent just can't remember what he said the first time around.

For example, we try to enforce a strict 7:30 bedtime, but sometimes activities keep us out until later, and after baths and all the other bells and whistles of bed preparation, it's 8:30 and everyone under three-feet tall is still roaming the house. Consistency dictates a story before bed every night, but it's already too late for that, and see how one domino out of place makes the whole structure topple? Oh, man, plus there are dominoes to pick up downstairs and clothes to lay out for tomorrow and . . .

Confucius thinks the key to consistency is to keep a closer eye on the clock.

COOLING-OFF PERIOD

DEFINITION

The cooling-off period, also known as a "positive time-out," is the time that a parent uses to put some space between him and his kid during a tantrum or outburst. This allows kids and parents a few moments to readjust emotionally in an attempt to find constructive solutions to issues and arguments.

Cooling-off periods are helpful to stop a negative behavior that has spun out of control because they give the child time to calm down and deal with his emotions. They also give parents a moment to cool off and avoid losing their tempers, which allows them to make an unemotional decision on the best way to deal with the problem and preserve a positive relationship with the child.

The cooling-off period is best used in a situation that involves a power struggle. For example, when the child is putting up a fight about eating dinner or going to bed. These types of situations tend to cause everyone's emotions to run high and can cause parents to make rash decisions involving their child. In these moments, parents or children are more likely to speak out of frustration, and extreme punishments often occur in retaliation. In response, kids tend to focus on seeking revenge instead of improving their behavior.

DADFINITION

A cooling-off period is the ringing of the bell in an MMA fight that signals the end of the round. During this time, both fighters should retire to their corners and think about what went wrong in that round and come out with their hands up in an attempt to hug. Yes, this would be an awful UFC fight, but it would make a fight between parent and child much easier to endure.

It's important to note that a cooling-off period is much different than a typical time-out. It's not necessary to make a kid stay in his room or in the corner for a specific amount of time. Taking a cooling-off period isn't a way to punish your child. Rather, it's a tool you can use to ensure both you and your child are able to manage your anger in an appropriate way.

Cooling-off periods are essential in the heat of battle with a child. He's saying things he doesn't mean, and you're getting angry and wondering if a life sentence in the basement is a harsh penalty. Everyone needs to chill the hell out. Kid on one end of the couch, dad on the other end, and no one says a word until his face is three lighter shades of red.

COPARENTING

DEFINITION

Coparenting describes any parenting situation where the mother and father are not married, living together, or in a romantic relationship with each other.

Adults who agree to coparent believe that their children should have stability and an equal relationship and equal access to both parents, no matter what situation the parents are in. During the first year of life, respectful, collaborative, organized coparenting has been shown to contribute to the growth of a well-adjusted child later in life, while the opposite is true of contentious, disorganized coparenting.

DADFINITION

Coparenting is a situation where mom and dad pretend to like each other for the sake of the children.

Coparenting, even if mom and dad are just pretending to tolerate one another, is obviously the healthier option when compared to the "every other weekend" parenting style popular in previous decades. With coparenting there's no verbally bashing the opposite parent or futilely attempting to become the favorite parent when you have the kid over Christmas break.

You'll run into far more couples who are coparenting than you ever imagined, but these couples won't always seem obvious. If you're looking for the coparenting couple in the crowd, just look for the mother and father who really get along and don't hang out together very often. Basically, look for the parents who seem happy.

CROUP

DEFINITION

Croup is an infection of the upper airway (mainly the windpipe and the voice box) that results in inflammation that causes hoarseness, a hacking cough, and obstructed breathing.

Viral croup is the most common type of croup and is also the type of croup most commonly experienced by kids between the ages of six months and three years. It can affect older kids as well. Most cases of viral croup sound worse than they are and can be treated at home with a cool mist humidifier, which helps break up anything that's hardened in the airway. Croup *can* be severe and even life threatening. While this is rare, call your doctor if you're concerned.

DADFINITION

Croup is categorized by a barking cough that you may not notice because kids cough *all the damn time!*

It seems like most kids are always either getting over being sick or about to get sick. If your kid goes to daycare, you know exactly what I mean. Daycare should be called the Croup Troop because kids spend half the day playing and the other half covering their mouth to cough.

If you suspect croup, take your kid to see a doctor, though most doctors won't see a kid unless there is a fever. Instead, call the doctor on his house phone at 2 A.M. and let him listen to the cough.

CRUISING

DEFINITION

One of the final stages of movement before walking, cruising is classified as a child moving upright around a room with the assistance of couches, tables, other humans, or any sturdy object used as a support and a means to get around.

Cruising usually begins with the child moving and shuffling her feet only a few inches at a time using her hands and eyes to steady her movements. After the child is comfortable with upright movement, she'll begin to pick up her feet and travel from location to location by reaching out for the next spot.

DADFINITION

Cruising is the baby doing her best impression of "daddy with a hangover"—clinging to chairs, family pets, and any seemingly sturdy surface as a means to get from point B to point C without falling flat on her point A.

Cruising does come with some major tumbles, so be ready to pick your kid up and assure her that everything is fine after she lands butt first on her toys, bumps head-on into pointy furniture, and just has her legs give out from the sudden weight placed on her not yet fully developed knees and legs.

To encourage cruising, try not to carry your baby as much as you did when he wasn't moving on his own, don't keep her confined to small areas like a playpen, and allow her to roam around the house freely. Just make sure you've sufficiently babyproofed the joint and remove all road-blocks on the floor like toys, clothes, and shoes.

You may also want to hold your baby's favorite toy or stuffed animal just far enough out of reach so that she has to cruise over to it—just like your partner does with the aspirin during your hangover cruising—and watch the little girl learn quick when it means getting what she wants.

DELAYED DEVELOPMENT

DEFINITION

"Delayed development" is a term used to describe either failure to attain the skills expected at a certain age—such as language skills, social skills, or motor skills—or the delayed attainment of those skills compared to other children of the same age. Doctors use guidelines set down by the American Academy of Pediatrics to diagnose delayed development, but parents often call delays out to their child's pediatrician.

DADFINITION

Delayed development is something every parent fears, but most don't have to be worried about. Every kid is different, and some kids develop faster or slower than others.

My first kid didn't start talking until he was almost two years old. Our pediatrician recommended bringing in assessors to see if there was a bigger issue. They ran him through a slew of tests. He passed them all. He just didn't feel like talking until a week after the assessment when he started yapping in complete sentences.

Delayed development is a common occurrence in children. Probably because doctors, specialists, and even parents themselves put a time-table on every important moment like the kid is training for a marathon and needs to hit certain split times. Your child needs to be cruising by this age, walking by this age, and should have a firm grasp on how to fix the water heater by the first grade. While delayed development is a real problem for some children, don't worry until it's clear that you have something to worry about.

EARLY INTERVENTION

DEFINITION

Early intervention is a system of government services that helps eligible babies and toddlers with disabilities, developmental delays, or potential developmental delays learn the basic skills that usually develop during the first three years of life. These skills include physical skills such as reaching, crawling, and walking; cognitive skills such as solving problems; communication skills like talking, listening, and comprehension; and social and emotional skills.

If an infant or toddler has a disability or a delay in one or more of these developmental areas, the child will likely be eligible for early intervention services. Most of the time, these services are available at low or no cost to the parent.

DADFINITION

Early intervention is helping kids help themselves when the child is progressing a little slower than other kids his age.

Early intervention is sometimes a dirty word, and some parents are embarrassed to admit their child is a part of early intervention classes. However, I'll be the first to admit my kid was tested for early intervention.

My firstborn was more than two years old and wasn't talking except for simple words. Early intervention sent in a group to test him.

He didn't end up needing the services, but many children do. It's nothing to be ashamed of at all. It's better to get help when it's first needed than when it might be too late.

EGOCENTRISM

DEFINITION

"Egocentrism" is a psychology term that refers to the belief of a child who assumes that other people experience the world in the same way that he does.

Egocentric children presume that their own concerns, values, and preoccupations are equally important to everyone else's. Egocentric thinking is often an overestimation of one's uniqueness, which often results in feelings of alienation or of being misunderstood.

DADFINITION

Egocentrism is the inability of a child to put himself in someone else's shoes—and boy do I know about a hundred adults suffering from the same affliction. I'll assume they're the kid's parents.

If a kid thinks the world revolves around him, there's a good chance that it does. If this sounds like your kid, maybe it's time to take a step back. Let your kid do things for himself and teach him that not everyone gets to take the trophy at the end of the game. If you think your child is egocentric, take comfort in the fact that egocentrism usually diminishes over time, largely as a consequence of interactions with other children and adults, and because not everyone will let the little guy get his way.

ELIMINATION COMMUNICATION

DEFINITION

Elimination communication, or EC, is also known as potty whispering, the way in which parents tune in to the verbal, physical, and emotional communications of their children to facilitate potty training.

Advocates of elimination communication, a term coined by author and elimination expert Ingrid Bauer, believe that training a baby to use the toilet can begin almost immediately from birth. Mothers using the elimination communication method leave their children bare bottomed and read interpersonal cues to guess when bowel movements will occur.

DADFINITION

Elimination communication is really giving a crap about the way your kids crap.

Elimination communication demands not only constant attention to avoid a major mess but a mental (or written) tracking of the kid's daily bowel movements. It's about as complicated as betting on sports.

Training a child to use the bathroom is a vital moment in the development of a child, and there could be major ramifications down the line if the child is forced to use a toilet too soon. Also, if you start training before the child is ready, the kid could put up major resistance, leading to a host of behavioral issues. Wait too long and the issues become internal and possibly mental. And let's not forget the pressure this puts on mom and dad—blink too long and the new couch might soon become the new guest bathroom.

EXPRESSIVE AND RECEPTIVE LANGUAGE

DEFINITION

"Expressive and receptive language" is the bucket term for all communication experienced by human beings. Language itself is broken down into two sections:

- Receptive language describes the words, communicated by others, that you hear and comprehend.
- Expressive language describes the words that you use to communicate your thoughts with others.

Language education plays a huge role in a child's life, and children begin to learn both types of language skills soon after birth. Children use these skills to become good listeners and good communicators throughout the rest of their lives. Children's receptive language skills develop more quickly than their expressive language skills, which means they're able to understand more than they can communicate. Some parents teach their children baby sign language as a way to communicate with their children until their expressive language skills catch up.

DADFINITION

All communication with kids between the ages of two and five is broken down into two sections—the "What the hell did you just say?" and the "Did you hear what the hell I just said?"

Your child will be learning new words and phrases but won't yet have mastered the pronunciation of those words. She'll get frustrated if you don't understand what she is trying to say, and you'll get frustrated because you're attempting to communicate with a drunk relative. I once had a five-minute conversation where I thought my kid was talking about someone named Lou when he was really saying the word "you."

It's vital to stop and correct your kid on the words that she gets stuck on the most—unless you want to sit at McDonald's and have an entire conversation about your good friend, Lou.

HELICOPTER PARENTING

DEFINITION

Helicopter parenting is a parenting style where parents "hover" over their children and are incredibly focused on and involved in their lives. Parents who practice helicopter parenting tend to be anxious about what would happen to their children if they weren't involved. They also tend to be overinvolved in their children's educational lives.

Although the term is most often applied to parents of teens who feel that their children are incapable of completing certain tasks alone, helicopter parents can have children of any age.

DADFINITION

Helicopter parenting is overparenting to the point of smothering.

Hovering above your kid like a news chopper over a high-speed chase doesn't prevent the kid's eventual crash and foot chase through a residential neighborhood. And, in fact, the feeling of constantly being under surveillance is incredibly prohibitive to the development of a young child.

A kid making decisions that aren't made due to a sense of what's right or wrong, but are made because dad is constantly watching, means that kid probably won't develop into a healthy, free-thinking adult. It just means she'll figure out other ways to avoid authority figures and do whatever she damn well pleases.

FICTIONAL BUT FUNNY

MOMTOURAGE

A group of moms who lean on each other for support and usually travel to functions in a cohesive group.

IMAGINARY FRIEND

DEFINITION

An imaginary friend is a companion or friend that a child creates in his mind. An imaginary friend does not exist in the real world.

It's very common for young children to have imaginary friends. Various psychological theories postulate that a child works through a variety of fears, anxieties, or even goals and a perception of the world through his relationship with his imaginary friend. Although imaginary friends may seem very real to their creators, children typically understand that the imaginary friend does not actually exist.

DADFINITION

An imaginary friend is the person your kid will trust the most, especially when things around the house get broken or go missing.

While very useful as scapegoats, imaginary friends are also incredibly helpful to kids to cope with new situations like school, moving, or another kid popping out of mom's belly and suddenly grabbing all of the attention. You can learn so much about what your kid is thinking and feeling by eavesdropping in on conversations with his imaginary friend. Just don't get caught.

Imaginary friends are perfectly normal up to a certain age. If your kid is still talking to fictional friends past the first grade, you might want to discuss the issue with a professional.

INDEPENDENT PLAY

DEFINITION

Independent play is play that allows a child to decide on her own how she'll play and what she'll play with, without any adult guidance.

Teaching a child how to play alone and abstaining from requests to join in the play make the child more independent and reliant on her own imagination for entertainment. Independent play is healthy because it teaches children to be creative during play time, apply critical thinking to the way they play, explore the ways to play, and even develop new interests and hobbies.

It's important for an adult to remain close during play time, and to keep the play environment safe so the child can't get into anything dangerous. During this time, you shouldn't hover over the child. Instead, use this time to do some of the tasks you haven't had time to accomplish because you're always caring for a young child.

DADFINITION

Getting a kid to play independently is a slow process that will make you feel like a horrible dad. The good thing is that independent play is learned over time—by both you and your child. You can't just dump a kid in the middle of a room with some toys and say, "Here, entertain yourself." You have to teach your child how to play and then allow her to take the reins.

That said, once your kid gets the hang of independent play, it won't always be good for you. There will be an immediate feeling of guilt in the moments after your kid requests that you, "Come play, daddy," and you refuse the request. Right after the guilt comes the worry that you're somehow screwing the kid up for the rest of her life because you didn't play beauty parlor with her that one time when she was five. If you feel this guilt, just remember that independent play is just as important to your child's development as it is to your sanity.

Independent play is healthy, but there is a difference between independence and avoidance. Try to find a balance between playing along with your kid and letting her do her own thing.

MANIPULATIVE TOYS

DEFINITION

Manipulative toys are toys that involve a child's cognitive skills and get little fingers and brains actively working together. They basically teach kids how to manipulate objects. These toys teach children fine motor skills and hand-eye coordination, and include items such as nesting cups, puzzles, busy books, and interlocking blocks. Other manipulative toys require kids to open and close doors and windows on a toy house, put shapes in a shape sorter, lace a shoe, or place smaller objects in various spots to correctly build objects such as a truck, animal, or building.

DADFINITION

Manipulative toys are best described as the toys most likely found at a doctor's office, preschool, or the bottom of a Christmas list as a very last resort. They are best for the baby's brain and thinking skills even if they're not the loudest, brightest, or most sought after toy in the toy store.

In addition, manipulative toys keep a child's imagination going while keeping you and mom a little bit heavier in the wallet. Why? Well, manipulative toys sometimes don't even have to be toys at all. Any item that can be opened and closed, stacked and unstacked, or used creatively by a kid is considered a manipulative toy. I'm not saying that you should cheap out and buy your kid a stack of shirt boxes for a birthday gift, but feel free to be creative in a pinch.

MATURE MAKE-BELIEVE

DEFINITION

Mature make-believe is a popular type of role-playing where a child uses her imagination to create a real-life scenario. For example, she'll pretend that a block is a phone if she's pretending to make a phone call or that a stick is a spoon if she's pretending to cook.

Mature make-believe is important because it is different from the typical "no rules" type of play that most toddlers are accustomed to, since it encourages kids to imagine themselves playing various roles and to create a pretend scenario based on possible, real-life instances. In mature make-believe, kids use the specific language that corresponds with that role.

Mature make-believe is an integral part of executive function development, which is sometimes referred to as self-regulation, and is a collection of mental processes that connect experiences from the past (such as time spent talking on the phone) to the action that's happening in the present (the child wants to pretend to talk on the phone during play time). Executive function is important as a child gets older as it is the mental process used for activities such as remembering details, time management, making plans, organization, and more.

This mature make-believe and the role-playing can extend for hours, days, and sometimes even weeks.

DADFINITION

Mature make-believe is the process of teaching a child to play pretend but to keep it as real as possible.

Take for example the popular kid's pretend scenario of playing doctor (not to be confused with the perverted teen version of playing doctor). In mature make-believe one kid will play the doctor, say everything a doctor would, use all of the equipment a doctor would, and hopefully charge the full amount a real doctor would (especially if he's your kid and you're trying to make the next mortgage payment). Another child would play the nurse (assist the doctor as a nurse would), and another would play the patient (pretend to be sick and skip out on the bill if he doesn't have medical insurance).

Mature make-believe is a positive way to encourage kids to play and gives a peek into their comprehension of how the world works. It's good once in a while. Occasionally kids must be encouraged to just let their minds roam when playing pretend. If a kid wants to be a doctor who can sew animal parts onto humans, so be it. The world needs creativity—and humans with octopus arms.

MODERN MOTHERING STYLES

DEFINITION

Modern moms are the new breeds of mothers caring for children across the country. Modern moms fall into three distinct categories based on their parenting style.

1. A **silky mom** is a woman who prefers a medicated hospital birth, splits the feeding into part-time breastfeeding and part-time formula feeding, uses only disposable diapers, insists on crib sleeping, and follows the advice of the established medical authority. Silky moms are working moms who prefer modern conveniences to make parenting easier.
2. A **crunchy mom** is a mother who exclusively breastfeeds and supports home birth, babywearing, cloth diapering, cosleeping, and gentle discipline. Crunchy moms tend to question established medical practices, eat exclusively vegan or vegetarian with all-organic foods, and are very aware of what goes into their child's, and their own, body.
3. A **scrunchy mom** is a combination of both mothering styles. A scrunchy mom might believe in only breastfeeding but doesn't believe a child should sleep in the same bed as the parents. She'll be conscious of food labels but will occasionally allow the child to eat junk food. A scrunchy mom does tend to lean heavily towards one style or the other.

DADFINITION

A modern mom is a woman who does what she feels is best for the baby and for her way of life. These three styles are as much a reflection on the way the modern mom feels about the Earth as they are on the way she believes a child should be raised.

It's easy to figure out what type of mom your partner will be well before the baby arrives. Is she a workaholic who will put as much passion into raising her child as she did climbing the ladder? Does she shop at Ann Taylor? Does she want both a family and a career? She's silky.

Did you meet your partner at a Phish concert? Did she try to talk you into naming your child after a Phish song? Does she look like the lead singer of Phish? She's crunchy.

Does your partner work incredibly hard and is on the fast track to management even though she spent every weekend of her twenties ripping bong hits in her Phish 2004 tour shirt while binge watching Bravo marathons? She's scrunchy.

NANNY

DEFINITION

A nanny is an individual who provides care for children in addition to the parents.

Unlike au pairs, nannies often have additional training in working with children and sometimes have a degree in child development. Nannies also usually live apart from the family and don't provide domestic help unless otherwise stated in the employment relationship. A nanny that helps with the housework is often referred to as a "mother's helper."

Nannies also work for short periods of time—usually in the hours before school or after school before parents get home from work. Nannies usually have lives and families of their own and don't often fraternize with the family outside of their daily duties.

Within the last few decades, the "manny" has grown in popularity, and it's exactly as it sounds—a man doing the job instead of a woman.

DADFINITION

Nannies are caregivers who provide another set of hands to help keep you afloat as you raise your kid. If you can afford in-home care, it's a much better alternative than the typical afterschool program.

The hardest part about finding a nanny is just that—finding a nanny. It's tough to find a person who not only fits all of your family's needs but also meshes well with your child. A nanny is almost like a third parent, so the child's comfort with the nanny is of utmost importance.

Another drawback to the nanny is the high turnover rate—nannies tend to leave if the situation isn't up to their standards, or the family expects more though they're not paying more. There are even cases of "nanny pilfering," which means another family has made a better offer and taken the nanny right out from under your nose.

It's vitally important that you do the research and find the right fit for your family. The rest is just all part of the parenting game.

ORGANIC

DEFINITION

Organic food is natural food that is grown or raised without the use of synthetic pesticides or fertilizers. Animal products that are labeled "organic" must be free of antibiotics and growth hormones and must come from animals that are fed organic feed and given access to the outdoors. Produce that is labeled "organic" cannot come from genetically engineered seeds.

According to findings from the Organic Trade Association, the organic food industry takes in over $30 billion in sales each year, proving that parents really do put in an effort to eat healthy and feed their children better food.

DADFINITION

Organic food is real food, without chemical engineering, that probably tastes delicious; however, the average person can't afford to buy organic.

Once you have a kid and really take a look at the ingredients inside your kid's favorite cereal, snack, and treat, you'll toss it in the trash immediately and swear off all processed foods. You'll run right out to the grocery store, pick up the organic versions of your normal store items, ring up at the register, and, once you realize you can't spend $300 on groceries, put it all back and grab the snacks back out of the trash.

Organic food is much better for your body but way worse for your wallet. If you're interested in eating organic, start growing crops in your backyard. Then sell those crops and use the money to shop at Whole Foods.

OVERPRAISE

DEFINITION

Overpraise is the habit of praising a child for a job well done, even when praise isn't necessary. Overpraise is often excessive and undeserved.

Parents who overpraise tend to focus on a kid's "greatness"—either real or fabricated—and make exaggerated statements that fail to reflect a kid's true abilities like mentioning how many goals their kid scored in a league where scores aren't kept.

When parents overpraise or overindulge kids, the children may start to form a sense of entitlement or expect life to be easy because they're "so great" at everything they do. This leaves them ill-prepared to face the eventual challenges in life outside the protective wall of praise.

DADFINITION

Overpraise is positive reinforcement on drugs . . . and it is doing your kids more harm than good. Sure, you want your kids to feel good about themselves, even in those moments when they weren't successful, but there is a huge difference between a "Nice try" and a "That was the most amazing thing you've ever done as a human," and many parents opt for expressing the latter.

Overpraise tends to overinflate the ego and makes kids feel that they don't need to try harder. Parents aren't the only people to blame for the overpraise epidemic. Grandparents who make it seem like the child is a walking messiah who farts rainbows, and sports leagues that reward participants with huge trophies just for stepping on the field, also contribute to this issue.

Self-esteem isn't created by telling a kid everything he does is perfect, because one day he's going to realize he can't do anything well at all, and where will you be then?

OVERSCHEDULING

DEFINITION

Overscheduling is the habit of enrolling kids in too many extracurricular activities—anything from sports and playdates to tutoring and music lessons—and filling up every moment outside of school with a learning experience.

Allowing kids to participate in extracurricular activities teaches them to work with others, plan and think constructively, and opens them to new experiences, but overscheduling doesn't allow children the time to do the important things that kids do in their free time.

The classic signs of an overscheduled child include a constant complaint that she is tired or doesn't feel right, schoolwork begins to suffer, the child is never just sitting around doing nothing, she shows no emotion or joy in the hobbies she once found fun, and she rejects outright some of her scheduled extracurricular activities.

FICTIONAL BUT FUNNY

FEAR OF MISSING OUT (FOMO)

A form of social anxiety, FOMO is the overpowering feeling that either you or your child are missing out on opportunities that may be enjoyable or satisfying. In adults, FOMO is the reason for constantly checking and updating Facebook, Twitter, e-mail, and other social networking services to provide constant feedback and an opportunity to compare your life to that of others. With children, FOMO is the reason the parents need to say yes to every party, playdate, and social event their child is invited to out of fear they'll be left out of other events in the future.

DADFINITION

The signs of an overscheduled child are obvious, if the kid is around the house long enough for a parent to notice.

Just as there are verbal and nonverbal indicators that will tell you if your child is overscheduled, there are telltale signs in your own life that make it obvious that this is an issue. If you're in a car, at a practice, at the mall buying items for a kid to participate in a planned activity, or just not at home at all anymore, your kid is doing too much. An overscheduled kid comes equipped with an overscheduling (and overscheduled) parent.

Overscheduling happens for two reasons: Either a parent is afraid his child is going to miss out on an opportunity if her day isn't filled with soccer practice, piano lessons, and additional math studies, or the parent regrets not taking part in those activities when he was a kid.

Kids need time to be kids just like parents need time where they're not shuttling those kids around. So do you and your child a favor and take the time you need to occasionally just veg out.

PARENTAL RIGHTS

DEFINITION

"Parental rights" refers to the right of the parents, foster parents, or in some cases the legal guardians to make important decisions on behalf of their child. These rights include the right to pass property to a child through inheritance, the right to make medical or educational decisions for that child, and the right to retain custody of the child.

Parental rights may be terminated if the parent or guardian has been proven to be unfit by the court.

DADFINITION

"Parental rights" means, until the age of eighteen, that kid belongs to you. You're in charge.

And with this responsibility comes all of the good, bad, awful, and awesome stuff that goes along with it. It's kind of what you expected when you and your partner became the decision-makers in charge of another human being's life.

No pressure at all my friend, no pressure at all.

PARENTING COACH

DEFINITION

A parenting coach is a professionally trained, knowledgeable individual who helps parents deal with the challenges of raising a child. A parenting coach builds a relationship with parents and helps them maintain a positive outlook, while also acting as a source of encouragement and compassion.

A parenting coach attempts to identify the strengths and weakness of the parents as it relates to raising a child and builds upon those strengths. A parenting coach will also offer a variety of suggestions on ways parents and children can interact to improve the family dynamic. Common issues that a parenting coach will address include constant power struggles between the parents and child, bedtime and sleeping issues, eating issues, temper tantrums, separation anxiety, and aggression.

DADFINITION

A parenting coach is the mentor parents turn to when they just don't know what the hell do to anymore.

Think of a child as a ticking time bomb, but one that can be defused—if you're familiar with bombs. Now imagine the bomb must be defused a different way every single time. It's impossible to always know the best way to handle every situation a kid can throw at a parent, but parenting coaches give families a variety of ways and responses to common issues. After all, you can't keep jumping on the bomb and hoping it doesn't take out an entire town.

Parenting coaches can be pricey (sometimes $100 an hour), but the honest assessment of your parenting skills and the suggestions to better handle your child are worth the price for a little sanity.

PERMISSIVE PARENTING

DEFINITION

Permissive parenting, also known as indulgent parenting, is a lenient parenting style where parents supply few and inconsistent rules and don't often discipline the child for misbehaving.

These parents are typically very loving and nurturing, but they tend to avoid confrontation with their children. Oftentimes, parents who practice permissive parenting use bribery to get their children to practice appropriate behavior.

DADFINITION

Permissive parenting is a parenting style where mom and dad act more like their kid's friend than an authority figure.

Permissive parents are often not grown-up enough themselves to handle the care of another human. And while the authoritative parent looks to run the house like a democracy, and the authoritarian parent is fine with a dictatorship, the permissive parent is content to live in a world of controlled anarchy.

While it's nice to feel like your child can tell you anything, and looks to you as a friend, it's not really in the best interest of the child to just be a buddy. It's fine to have a close relationship, but a kid needs a parent more than he needs another friend.

PLAYDATE

DEFINITION

A playdate is an arranged day and time set up by parents for children to get together for a few hours of supervised play.

Scheduled playdates, which are a way to make sure a child socializes with kids her own age, have become common due to the hectic life and work schedules of parents. Playdates can be held either in the home or at a kid-friendly location such as a museum, park, or zoo. They are typically coordinated with daycare friends or sports friends as a way for kids to interact outside of the strict confines of school or athletic activities.

DADFINITION

There's an old expression that says "You can't pick your kid's friends." But this expression is misleading. Thanks to the playdate, you may not be able to choose the child that your kid will want to hang out with, but you can prevent your kid from hanging out with the child. Especially if the kid's parents are unbearably, mind-numbingly boring.

Playdates are fantastic because they occupy your kid for a couple of hours. However, they become torturous if the other parents exhibit

FICTIONAL BUT FUNNY

BABY SHAM

Whether a get-together is officially a "Congratulations, you've had the baby!" party or toddler tea party, a baby sham is a way to pretend that the celebration is for your little one when it's really about getting adults together to drink.

all the personality of a bag of wet sand. Just remember that there's nothing wrong with setting up playdates for your kids based on the parents you'd want to hang out with. You're essentially using your kid as a connection to cooler couple friends. It's harmless. You're going to use your kid for way worse things in the next few years.

POSITIVE DISCIPLINE

DEFINITION

Positive discipline is a discipline model that focuses on the positive points of behavior. It is based on the belief that there are no bad children, just good and bad behaviors exhibited by kids.

Parents enact positive discipline by modeling the behaviors they want their children to embrace. For example, if parents want their children to not yell or throw a tantrum when they become frustrated, the parents need to refrain from yelling or losing their patience when they become frustrated as well. Basically, positive discipline is a way for parents to teach their kids how to behave by behaving in certain ways themselves.

DADFINITION

Positive discipline is a strategy that forces parents to behave themselves—even if they *really* don't want to.

Basically, monkey see, monkey do. If your go-to technique to handle any situation is to display anger and yell, you can expect to see the same behavior from your child. If that's the way you react to his bad behavior, he will only act out more.

If you're going to practice positive discipline, you need to attempt to do the following:

- Understand the meaning behind your child's behavior.
- Be consistent with your expectations of your child.
- Give attention to the behavior you like and not focus on the behavior you don't.

- Redirect your child's focus instead of drawing attention to the bad behavior by telling him, "No, don't do that!"
- Focus on controlling yourself and not your child.

If you use positive discipline, your mantra should be "There are no bad kids, only bad behaviors; there are no bad parents, only a bad reaction to kids acting out."

POTTY TRAINING

DEFINITION

Potty training is the process of teaching a child how to use the toilet so she can transition from wearing diapers to wearing underwear.

Training usually starts with a small, toilet-bowl-shaped device—known as a potty—but once the child is comfortable to go on her own, she transitions to an adult toilet.

Most children will control their bowel movements before they're able to control their bladders, so training a child to urinate when necessary is usually a much easier task. The appropriate time for potty training depends on the maturity of the particular child, but most toddlers are ready to begin around the age of two or two and a half. Girls tend to be ready for potty training before boys and will learn to stay dry overnight in a shorter amount of time as well.

DADFINITION

Potty training is the final step to parental freedom. Sort of.

After a while, changing, disposing of, and buying diapers becomes a real pain in the ass. Ironic, isn't it, that this particular pain in the ass involves that specific body part on a child? A potty-trained child means no more handling the feces of another human being. Picking up after a dog is one thing, but carrying around the crap of a child because there's no place to toss it becomes demeaning to even the most confident parent.

Once a child learns to recognize her need to move her bowels, goes into the bathroom herself, handles her business and the cleanup, and doesn't get her own poop all over the place, it's time to celebrate.

PRODUCT RECALL

DEFINITION

A product recall is the request from a manufacturer to return a product to the store or receive a manufacturer-sanctioned fix after safety issues have been discovered. These safety issues or product defects may put the user in danger and put the maker at risk for legal action.

Recalls are costly for a company, and a company that recalls items after death or injury—especially of children—risks the loss of public trust. In addition, the manufacturer has to fix or replace the recalled product and is held financially responsible for any injuries or other consequences.

DADFINITION

Product recalls are another way for companies to admit they've made a big piece of junk, a big piece of junk that costs a ton of money.

It's important to pay attention to product recalls because some strollers, cribs, and toys pose a threat to your kid. If any of the products you use to care for your child are recalled, return the products immediately and ask for a refund. Don't wait for another similar product that's going to break or just get recalled again. Shop around for another item from a different manufacturer.

Even if a stroller or crib isn't recalled, feel free to return it to the store if you feel it's a threat to your child's safety. It's best not to wait until something bad happens.

REDSHIRTING

DEFINITION

Academic redshirting is the practice of postponing a child's entrance into kindergarten in order to allow extra time for emotional, intellectual, or physical growth. This occurs most frequently in cases where a kid's birthday is close to the cutoff date for enrollment, and putting the child into school at that point will mean she'll be one of the youngest kids in her class.

"Redshirting" is derived from a college term that describes the process of holding athletes back from playing sports in order to give them a physical advantage. The term "redshirt" refers to the actual red shirts that those athletes wear in practices and scrimmages.

DADFINITION

Up to this point, sports analogies have been used to explain some parenting terms, but "redshirting" is a parenting term that actually has a real sports meaning!

Redshirting has benefits and drawbacks. Research has shown that children who enroll in school later have greater academic successes, but the advantages tend to fade away once children reach the higher grades. Other studies have shown that while kids who are older than their classmates are usually more popular because of social confidence, those same students became discipline problems in later years.

According to the National Center for Education Statistics, recent studies have shown it's actually the youngest students who tend to excel in classroom settings.

You could be damned if you hold her back one more year or damned if you put her in school among kids much older. Damn, this parenting thing never gets easier.

SIPPY CUP

DEFINITION

A sippy cup is a cup that allows children to drink without spilling. Today's sippy cups are usually made out of BPA-free plastic and feature screw-on lids with a variety of spouts.

Sippy cups help a baby transition from nursing or bottle feeding to using a regular cup. They can also help your baby learn and improve developmentally appropriate skills like hand-to-mouth coordination and a growing sense of independence.

Some children are able to use a sippy cup at six months of age, while others won't be interested until after their first birthday.

DADFINITION

A sippy cup is a cup made to hold drinks that fit perfectly in the hands of humans incapable of holding drinks.

Not all sippy cups are made the same. Most will claim to be spill-proof but will spill all over your newly cleaned carpet if a kid just walks past it holding his sippy cup. Most will claim to be airtight but will spill over even as you're attempting to screw on the lid. Most sippy cups are pieces of plastic crap.

If you do find the rare cup that doesn't spill, leak, or make a giant mess with little effort from the kid, buy as many as possible and rotate them frequently to prevent overuse.

Also, don't get sippy cup lazy—dump out the contents often, especially if they've been sitting out all day, and wash frequently or replace with a clean cup at least every other day. And never run a black light over a sippy cup. It'll make a hotel bedspread look like a hospital surgery room floor.

SLOW PARENTING

DEFINITION

Slow parenting, which is also called free-range parenting, is a parenting style in which children are encouraged to slow down and explore the world and their surroundings at a natural pace, instead of racing from one planned activity to the next. Parents who practice this style seldom organize activities for their children, instead allowing them to follow their own interests and really connect with their personal interests and family members.

DADFINITION

Slow parenting is an attempt to raise children as if it were 1940.

Much like the other parenting styles, there are positives and negatives to the slow-parenting style. The slow-parenting style encourages creativity and free play and doesn't rely on TV or handheld electronics to entertain a bored kid. The negative is the fact that a free-range kid moves at a slightly slower pace in a world that crushes people who don't adapt to a "moving every minute" mentality.

There is a balance that can be found between a day jam-packed with activities every second the child is awake as opposed to a life spent sitting on a backyard swing and staring into the sky for eight hours. Maybe ask the kid what activities he'd like to participate in, instead of taking the "sign up now, ask him later" approach to filling up his free time.

SMART VERSUS EDUCATIONAL TOYS

DEFINITION

A smart toy is a toy that gets "smarter" as play progresses due to on-board electronics. As the user moves along in play, the game adapts to adjust to the player's ability and skill level.

An educational toy is a toy that promotes learning along with fun play. These toys promote the education of the child intellectually, emotionally, or physically (in some cases all three) and assist the child in learning a particular subject or skill.

Many people confuse smart toys with educational toys, but they are often very different in both play and the experience they provide to users.

DADFINITION

Smart toys and educational toys are items that guarantee an overcrowded house. You'll find them strewn around the floor along with dumb toys and things that your children love to play with that aren't even really toys at all. If you ever try to toss any of these toys out (even if they haven't been touched in months), your kids will toss you out soon after.

Child development experts prefer educational toys over smart toys because they offer "open-ended" play. Classic toys such as LEGO and building blocks, baby dolls, toy cars and construction vehicles, and even stuffed animals allow kids to create different scenarios and situations with the toys, even though the toy itself remains the same. Though these toys aren't specifically "educational," they do call for kids to create, think, and act out in order to remain entertained.

As a parent, you'll probably prefer educational toys because they're a hell of a lot cheaper and your kids won't get tired of them as quickly as they do smart toys.

SNOWPLOW PARENT

DEFINITION

Snowplow parents are parents who, in the same way a snowplow pushes snow, try to muscle any and all obstacles out of the path of their children. The obstacles can be anything—from school work to uncooperative teachers and coaches and even other kids—but whatever is perceived as being an obstacle will be plowed away in an attempt to ensure their children do not fail. A few classic examples of snowplow-parenting techniques include parents approaching an administrator at school to get their kid's classroom changed because his friend is in another class, trying to bribe a coach in exchange for more playing time for their kid, or completing a child's homework assignment for him without the child even being present to do the work.

As with parents who overpraise, snowplow parents aren't really doing their kids any favors. Instead, their kids are left unprepared to fend for themselves when they reach adulthood.

DADFINITION

Snowplow parents are very much like another tool used to remove snow from a specific area. Here's another hint—both blow very hard.

It's fitting that parents who'll do anything to remove obstacles from their kid's path are called snowplow parents because think of the typical snowplow and all of the other work it creates just to remove a pile of snow. Sure, the snow is moved from one spot, but it's pushed into other areas where it just has to be moved again (like the end of your driveway . . .).

The same goes for snowplow parents. Sure, they get one issue out of their kid's way, but more issues just pile up as they go.

SQUATTING

DEFINITION

Squatting is a posture where the body's weight is on the feet but the knees are bent.

At around the age of one, children will instinctively begin to squat to get stuff off the ground instead of bending over to pick objects up. To move their development along, when the child begins to stoop over for a toy, show him how to bend at the knees into a squatting position. Keep in mind that younger children often need to hold onto something to stand up again.

DADFINITION

Squatting is a natural movement that is comfortable for children but is awful on the knees and legs of dads.

Squatting will help you notice how really out of shape you've become, because when you squat down to help your kid clean up toys or for him to show you something he found, you'll become pretty damn uncomfortable. That said, squatting is, however, slightly more comfortable than sitting on the floor because your ass won't automatically fall asleep. It's also light years better than kneeling; one long kneel and you might never get up. I actually haven't been able to transition from kneeling to a standing position smoothly in more than four years. I wrote this entire book kneeling in my living room, wishing I had the squatting skills of a one-year-old.

STAYCATION

DEFINITION

A staycation is a period of time off from work and school spent largely within driving distance of the home. Instead of one long trip spent in a distant city and hotel, a family opts to take day trips to amusement parks, zoos, festivals, and museums and save money on airfare and lodging and the typical expenses that accompany a destination vacation.

The earliest use of the term occurred in a 2003 article in the *Sun News*, and the term grew in popularity during the summer of 2008 when gas prices reached record highs, forcing families to reduce travel expenses.

DADFINITION

A staycation is a nice escape from the typical family vacation because, as you'll learn the very first time you take your child on vacation, vacations aren't really vacations any longer. When kids are involved, vacations become work because of all the preparation and details involved in even the simplest trip. The best way to recover from a family vacation is another vacation, minus the kids.

Staycations are cost-effective, but just like everything else in life they do come with drawbacks. First, the appeal of a destination vacation is being away from not just home but all of the thoughts and responsibilities of home. For a week, home life doesn't exist, but with a staycation, you're never really away from home for longer than eight to ten hours. The worries of home creep back in after the day is done. So, while staycations are nice every once in a while, you probably don't want to make one a summertime tradition. Because, even if you're still parenting when you're away on vacation, at least you got the hell out of the house.

TANTRUM

DEFINITION

A tantrum is a child's emotional outburst, which is usually characterized by displays of stubbornness, screaming, crying, angry words or actions, defiance, or, in some cases, physical violence toward others.

Once a tantrum starts, it's often impossible for a parent to get the child to stop, just as it's often impossible for the child to make it stop. But, while tantrums are incredibly unpleasant for parents—especially in public—they're even worse for the child. During the outburst, the child is often overwhelmed by his own internal rage or frustration. He's terrified by the angry emotions and the inability to control the outburst even if he wanted to.

DADFINITION

A tantrum is what happens when the rage and frustration inside of your child comes screaming out in a whirlwind of tears, yells, and fist pounding. This usually occurs when you're in your local supermarket with a full cart.

There is an amazing amount of rage inside every human. Some people are much better at controlling it than others. As we get older, we learn to remain in control or just not put ourselves in a situation that could cause a sudden spike in anger. Unfortunately, kids can't keep it all bottled up inside and release it during a gym session on a punching bag. As soon as anger hits, it's go time.

While there is little you can do to stop a tantrum, there are tricks you can try to keep one from occurring or to keep it from getting worse. You'll learn those on the fly, and you'll soon find out that yelling, screaming, physical and verbal abuse, or throwing a tantrum of your own isn't going to solve anything. Keep your head even when the kid temporarily loses his.

TIME-OUT

DEFINITION

Time-out is a pediatrician-recommended form of punishment where a child is removed from the environment where she behaved inappropriately. This technique generally involves quarantining a child in a corner or designated space where the child is instructed to stand or sit for a specific amount of time.

Time-out is a form of negative reinforcement. It teaches children that their inappropriate behavior won't be tolerated and that they can remain in the room with the distraction or person that caused them to act out until they're able to behave appropriately.

Originally a form of discipline used only in the home, time-outs are now acceptable behavioral procedures in schools, clinics, and hospitals.

DADFINITION

Time-out is a way to remove your kid from a potential or already-occurring meltdown. In most cases, the time-out accelerates the meltdown until the child has no other choice but to sit down and chill the hell out.

Time-outs are much different now than when we were children. For example, my kid's school encourages him to sit down and write down his feelings about being put into a time-out and the steps he'll take next time to prevent the situation. When I was younger, my mother would put me in the corner and smack my ass while I yelled, "Time-out, mom, time-out!"

So, if you want to keep your cool with your kid, practice the time-out technique. It's better in the long run for everyone involved.

TREE NUT ALLERGIES

DEFINITION

Tree nut allergies are the most common food allergies among children. Tree nuts include walnuts, hazelnuts, almonds, pistachios, cashews, and Brazil nuts. It's possible to be allergic to only one of these nuts, but it's suggested that kids who suffer from a tree nut allergy stay away from all nuts as a precaution. Note that peanuts are often lumped into this group, even though they are legumes, because of the chance they came in direct or indirect contact with a tree nut during the manufacturing process.

The allergic reactions to nuts can range from mild or severe and can happen instantly or not until hours after exposure or ingestion. A few signs that your kid might have a tree nut allergy include skin rashes, stomach cramps, vomiting, diarrhea, respiratory issues similar to allergies, and even lightheadedness. In the most severe cases, a child will suffer from anaphylaxis in which his blood pressure drops, breathing passages narrow, and his tongue swells.

DADFINITION

Although it will feel like every kid is allergic to something, tree nut allergies seem to be the most common allergy out there. Tree nut allergies are a lifelong issue, but recent studies have shown that approximately 9 percent of kids with a tree nut allergy can eventually outgrow the condition.

Food manufacturers are also sensitive to the issue and will clearly state whether a food contains a tree nut or if the food came in contact with a tree nut during manufacturing or packaging.

After a tree nut allergy is diagnosed, you'll have to carefully select what foods you keep in the house and plan to avoid exposure when your child is away from home. Most schools now encourage nut-free meal plans, and restaurants will explain on their menu if food is cooked in peanut oil.

VASECTOMY

DEFINITION

A vasectomy is a medical procedure where the vas deferens, the narrow tube that connects the testicles to the urethra, is clamped (no-scalpel) or cut (conventional) from each testicle to prevent sperm from mixing with the liquid that is released during ejaculation. After the procedure, the testicles continue to produce sperm, but it gets reabsorbed into the body.

A vasectomy is a safe, outpatient procedure and is considered a permanent form of male birth control. Most vasectomies take less than a half-hour to perform and, while uncomfortable, do not cause significant pain.

DADFINITION

Perhaps not as permanent a form of birth control as those tight jogging pants from college that you still slap on from time to time, the vasectomy is fast becoming the solution to the accidental baby.

You probably know an accidental kid. You might even be an accident. If the next closest sibling in your family moved away to college before you finished preschool, you were a mistake. A "happy accident" is the term parents use when they don't want to call their child a mistake to his face.

While accidents can be happy, vasectomies are painless and you'll be up and around in no time. Or

> ### FICTIONAL BUT FUNNY
>
> #### OOPSIE BABY
>
> A child that showed up even though you and your partner weren't necessarily trying.

you could milk it for all it's worth. There's a good chance your partner is the one forcing you to clip your nuts because she doesn't feel like popping birth control pills for the rest of her life, so put that guilt to good use. I'm no doctor, but a couple of days on the couch watching every single episode of *Dr. Who* doesn't sound like a bad little vacation from kid duty.

AFTERWORD

By this point, you know the words you need to keep in the back of your mind as you move through your partner's pregnancy, into the first year of your kid's life, and into the toddler years and beyond. You need to know this info in order to be the best dad you can be, but in order to make sure you accomplish this goal, you need to spend some time focusing on yourself, too. With that in mind, here are eleven things that every new dad should know right from the start.

YOU'RE A DAD EVEN BEFORE THE KID SHOWS UP

Daddy duty doesn't start on the day of your child's birth. There is a ton of preparation even before the kid makes his grand entrance. There are rooms to prepare, things to shop for, and an entire house to babyproof (because you're not going to have time once the child arrives). Also, an unborn baby starts to develop his hearing at sixteen weeks. He'll hear mom's voice 24/7, but make sure the baby hears you, too. Just make sure to let mommy know what you're doing. She'll find it odd that you're constantly pressing your face against her pregnant belly and talking if you don't clue her in.

YOU'RE NOT THE FIRST DAD TO THINK HAVING A KID WAS A MISTAKE

I don't want to sound cold, but this much is true—for the first few months of your kid's life you're going to spend a lot of time saying to yourself, "This was all a huge mistake." Now, let me be clear: The child is never the mistake, but the idea that you're mentally and physically prepared to care for another human being can seem like a big joke once you're actually in the trenches. Here's a truth—you're *never* ready. You're never physically ready. You're never emotionally ready. And, unless you're pulling in a boatload of dough, hand over fist, you're sure as hell never financially ready. But despite all that, kids are never a mistake. One day, probably not long after your kid is born, you'll admit to friends, strangers, and anyone who asks about your son or daughter that having a kid was the smartest thing you've ever done.

YOU'LL HAVE REGRETS ABOUT YOUR KIDS FOR MOST OF YOUR LIFE

Regret will creep in almost immediately after the child is born. It's not the regret of having a child but more the regrets of all the time you "wasted" before the kid arrived. You'll regret not spending more time for yourself, doing more things for yourself (or even as a couple), and not taking a little more time to focus on your own life and goals. Bad news—you're always going to have regrets in life. Those regrets are just a reflection on the choices you made or didn't make. People never sit back and reflect on the intelligent choices they've made in life. Humans love beating themselves up for the things they did or didn't do. Let it go.

YOU'RE GOING TO GET DEPRESSED, SO TALK TO SOMEONE ABOUT IT

For the first couple of months, people are going to look for any signs of depression in mom. Postpartum depression is a very serious issue among new mothers, but take it from a guy who's been in the situation—depression after childbirth is a very real issue with men, too. It's usually a combination of a drastic change of life and responsibilities and a severe lack of significant sleep. If you're feeling depressed in the least, talk to someone about those feelings. Tell your partner, tell your best friend, confide in a dad who's been in your position not too long ago. Don't bottle it up inside.

YOUR OLD LIFE IS OVER—BUT THE NEW LIFE WON'T BE AS BAD AS YOU'RE IMAGINING

Life will never be the same again, but when has your life ever remained exactly the same? College, new jobs, dating, engagement, married life, and whatever big milestones that you've hit have all been significant shifts in your existence. This is just one more change.

Now, for the first few years of your child's life, your life is going to be a hundred times more chaotic and stressful. It'll probably feel like you're trying to sprint in five feet of water. The farther you get, the more the waves of life push you back. That said, it's not as bad as it sounds. In your later years, you'll take it all back in a second, without thinking it over for a moment. Ask your dad if he'd do it all again.

NOT EVERYTHING YOU DO WILL SCREW UP YOUR KID FOR LIFE

Most parents make a promise to themselves, and silently to their child, that they won't do all of the things their parents did to "screw up" their own kid. It feels like a healthy approach, but it's actually more a projection of your own issues and insecurities. You obviously don't want to see those mirrored back in your own kid. The thing is, it's impossible to know how your kid is going to turn out because both nothing and everything, and I mean *everything*, you do affects her. You just don't know the severity. So don't worry about it. You have to raise your child the best way you know how.

DON'T CARE ABOUT OTHER PEOPLE WATCHING AND JUDGING

Every time I took the kids out in public, and especially when they were around other parents or even my own family, I'd feel as though I was being analyzed for the way in which I handled my child. It felt like a panel of judges were critiquing my performance, but I never got to hear their scores or comments. Eventually, I learned that people probably *are* watching, critiquing, and judging my performance as a dad. I also learned not to give a crap. Really, who cares what other people think about you? You know you're a good parent and that's the most important judgment of all. Well, your partner counts, too, but she'll probably tell you if you're doing an awful job.

NEVER TURN DOWN AN OFFER OF HELP

Relatives, friends, and neighbors are going to want to babysit, help with chores around the house, bring your family meals, and offer countless services to ease the burden of caring for a newborn. I cannot stress this enough—take any and all offers of help. Wars were never won with one soldier. Cities weren't built by one man. The more people who lend a hand, the less of a burden is put on the shoulders of the new mom and dad. Don't feel like less of a person, or less of a parent, for accepting help, and don't ever be afraid to ask for it either.

ONE KID IS GREAT, TWO FEELS LIKE TEN, AND THREE IS INSANE

This is a piece of advice for the fathers planning to have more than one child and even those who swear it's "one and done." Kids are hard, and adding a second after the first child makes things seem more than twice as hard. That said, while adding another kid (and then another) makes life much more difficult, it also makes it infinitely more rewarding. Just make sure you're ready to add another, or possibly two, after you've got the care for the first kid down to a science. If you're hell-bent on more than three kids, you're either a masochist or a saint. You'll be too busy to explain which.

IT GETS BETTER—THEN WORSE—THEN BETTER (AND THIS GOES ON FOR YEARS)

When your newborn starts sleeping regularly, eating properly, and adhering to a schedule, you're going to think, "This isn't so bad!" Then one day the naps will disappear; it will be a struggle to get the kid to ingest anything not coated in sugar; and you won't know the difference between day and night, east and west. Things will get easier before they get harder, and then they'll feel impossible before they go back to manageable. Life will never be perfect, but it will never feel unlivable. No matter what's going on, just remember that this, too, shall pass.

YOU'RE THE DAD AND NOT THE BACKUP QUARTERBACK

Mothers are amazing. The moment the child is born it feels as though mom knows what to do, when to do it, and how to handle a baby that demands so much. It's as though she spent years preparing when really it's all just instinct. Because mom seems to have everything under control, much like a quarterback on a successful team, it's easy for some dads to stand on the sideline and hold the clipboard. This is where I play the aggressive coach, smack the clipboard out of your hand, and bark in your face with Gatorade-scented breath, *"Get your butt out on the field and contribute!"*

Your partner isn't the quarterback and you're not the inexperienced backup. If sports analogies help, imagine you and your partner as a two-headed running attack. She's the halfback picking up the large chunks of yardage, while you're the fullback getting the tough carries for the first down or over the goal line. (Note—your child is not the ball. Please don't spike your child when you score.)

So now that you know what you're in for, take a deep breath and head into the fray. You've got this. I promise!

INDEX

reflux, 122
rooting, 123
separation anxiety, 125
"soft spot," 100
startle reflex, 112, 131
stork bites, 129–30
supplies for, 75
swaddling, 131
talking to, 206
teething, 132
tests, 69
tummy time, 133
umbilical cord, 60
umbilical stump, 61
vernix, 62
weaning, 136
Baby bauble, 51
Baby blues, 71–72, 207
Baby carriers, 74
Baby concierge, 20
Baby formula, 103
Baby gate, 145
Baby lotion, 73
Babyproofing home, 80–81
Baby sham, 186
Baby sign language, 146
Babywearing, 74, 139
Bacterial infections, 138. *See also*
  Illnesses
Bassinet, 75
Bathroom habits, 165, 190
Bathroom talk, 147–48
Bauer, Ingrid, 165
Bellybutton, 61

Birth
  assisted birth, 19
  birthing ball, 21
  breech presentation, 24
  Cesarean section, 26
  dilation, 25
  doula, 27
  effacement, 25
  epidural, 29
  episiotomy, 30
  Lamaze method, 43
  natural childbirth, 29, 46
  placenta, 42, 50, 60
  plan for, 22, 27, 37
  preparing for, 20, 22, 27, 206
  push present, 51
  triage, 55–56
  umbilical cord, 60
  umbilical stump, 61
  vernix, 62
  water birth, 63
Birth cord, 60
Birthing ball, 21
Birthing center, 39, 44, 63. *See also*
  Hospital
Birth plan, 22, 27, 37
Bonding, 71, 74, 94, 105, 133, 140,
  155
Booster seats, 149–50
Bowel movements, 108, 165, 190
Braxton Hicks contractions, 23. *See
  also* Contractions
Breast abscess, 76
Breastfeeding

ABOUT THE AUTHOR

Chris Illuminati is a writer, humorist, and dad. He's the creator of the popular parenting blog *Message with a Bottle*. When he's not making fun of parenting issues on Post-it notes, Chris is a senior editor at BroBible.com.